AGAINST ALL ODDS

A Memoir

AGAINST ALL ODDS

A Memoir

Tristian Smith

Against All Odds
A Memoir
© 2024 by Tristian Smith

Printed in the United States of America.
ISBN-13:
979-8-9908889-0-6 Paperback
979-8-9908889-1-3 Hardcover
979-8-9908889-2-0 eBook
LCCN: 2024912449

Photo Credit:
The Art Incubator
Taylor Burris
@theaihubkc
www.theaihubkc.org

Typeset by Ruchir Gupta

TWS Publishing
Manhattan, Kansas

Table of Contents

Dedication

To Preston—this book is just as much your story as mine; hope you enjoy it. I love you.

To Lisa, Kuumba, Oba, and Makeda—thank you for welcoming an 18 year-old chubby and traumatized kid into your home and your family seventeen years ago. I love every one of you.

To Samuel Wright, Nate Moore, Nick Landers, Aaron Penix-Bagby—We may not talk all the time, but I check you guys out on your IG and Facebook pages and I am proud of each of you. We will always be tied together from our time at Fort Valley State University. It is a privilege to call you friends.

To Shari Hatcher (RIP), Emma & Edward Stokes (RIP), Tonya & Sammie Burts, Ann & Eric Wyatt, Mary McFolley, Nora Carter, James Snell, Angela Payne-Davis, Nartasha Davis—It takes a village to raise a child and you all collectively have contributed to my success as a former foster youth and my growth as a man. You each respectively represent how caseworkers and foster parents should invest into and mold foster youth. Thank you all.

Foreword

Transitions mark the intersections of endings and beginnings, casting us into moments ripe for profound reflection on the intricate trajectory from our past to the vast potential of our future. As you venture into the forthcoming pages, Tristian Smith extends a heartfelt invitation, urging you to join him in a deeply personal exploration sparked by his recent transition from the military to civilian life. This pivotal juncture compelled Tristian to navigate the intricate tapestry of his own childhood, unraveling the complexities woven into the fabric of growing up in foster care.

My initial connection with Tristian unfolded through the digital corridors of LinkedIn, where our shared dedication to advocating for the well-being of youth sparked a purposeful dialogue. As a fervent advocate for youth myself, having recently transitioned from 25 years of leadership in child welfare to the unexplored realms of an untethered author, speaker, and consultant, Tristian's journey struck a resonant chord within me.

In "Follow the Love," my own expedition into the vital realms of youth voice integration and the championing of permanent connections for youth in care has revealed the transformative power embedded in narratives akin to Tristian's. His audacious decision to share his experiences within "Against All Odds" serves not only as a literary guide but as a luminous beacon, leading us through the intricate terrain of resilience and self-discovery.

Tristian's story transcends the personal; it emerges as a testament to the indomitable spirit capable of arising from the crucible of life's most formidable challenges. As we embark on this shared journey with Tristian, may his words become a wellspring of inspiration in the face of adversity, and may his reflections serve as a compass, guiding us toward a future where the voices of youth in care are not only heard but celebrated.

Within these pages, Tristian candidly walks readers through the poignant chapters of his life — from the profound loss of his mother to the darkest days he encountered, leading to a triumphant college graduation and Army Officer commission from Fort Valley State University. Baring his soul, Tristian shares his experiences so that those who come after him — foster youth, case managers, foster parents, and the system of care — can glean wisdom from his story of loss, pain, and, above all, resilience.

So, get ready to experience a tumultuous journey while reading this book. Some passages may be triggering, so approach with empathy and understanding. Tristian's narrative emerges as not just a personal testimony, but a beacon of insight for all who engage with it — a compelling call to learn from the struggles and triumphs of one individual's journey through the foster care system.

"Against All Odds" encapsulates the essence of succeeding when the odds seemed insurmountable. As a passionate youth advocate, I yearn for a day when every young person faces a world that believes in their potential and champions their resilience; a day when the phrase "Against All Odds" becomes a testament to the unyielding spirit that propels individuals to rise above challenges and shape their destinies.

Dr. Elizabeth Wynter

Dr. Elizabeth Wynter, an award-winning visionary, has dedicated over two decades to reforming child welfare policies and practices, tirelessly advocating for change. Her unwavering resolve motivates others to join the quest for an inclusive and supportive child welfare system. Dr. Wynter's pioneering initiatives, notably National Foster Youth Voice Month, challenge stereotypes by reshaping perceptions of youth from passive recipients to essential organizational assets. In her influential book, "Follow the Love," she charts a path for agencies to embrace youth voices and establish lasting connections. Known as the Foster Youth Voice Whisperer, Dr. Wynter empowers both youth and professionals to craft policies, programs, and practices that foster inclusivity, leaving an indelible mark on society's perception of vulnerable youth.

My Mission

This book is dedicated to the over 400,000 young souls navigating the complexities of the foster care system. Your journey, marked by trials that many cannot begin to fathom, stands as a testament to resilience and the indomitable human spirit. My story, laid bare in these pages, is a tribute to the exceptional individuals who illuminated my path during my darkest days, guiding me through tumultuous battles with my inner demons. It is a beacon of hope, intended to light your way through the shadows.

Your experiences, though marred by abuse, neglect, drug addiction, or the profound loss of a parent, are not definitions of your worth nor predictors of your future. Despite these formidable challenges, you possess the extraordinary capability to sculpt your destiny. A future replete with purpose, discipline, and inspiration is within your reach, should you choose to seize it. You are equipped to conquer the adversities at your doorstep, to defy the odds, and emerge with a story that not only celebrates survival but serves as an inspiration to the world at large.

Success is not a distant dream but a reality waiting to be realized through wise decisions, the company of those who uplift you, and, importantly, the humility to heed their advice. This book aims to arm you with lessons learned from personal experience — strategies to navigate life's storms and emerge victorious. My sincerest wish is for you to find solace and strength in these pages, allowing them to guide you towards a life marked by achievement and happiness.

To the educators, caregivers, and mentors — this narrative extends beyond the personal. It is a resource, a tool in understanding the unique challenges faced by those under your care. It underscores the significance of empathy, support, and the powerful role you play in shaping the futures of these young individuals.

This dedication is an invitation to share your journey. Your testimony, much like mine, has the power to light the way for others. In sharing our stories, we create a tapestry of hope and resilience, a collective narrative that speaks to the triumph of the human spirit over adversity. Whether through written word, dialogue, or any medium that resonates with you, I encourage you to share your story. In doing so, we foster a community of understanding, support, and mutual growth.

The journey toward healing and fulfillment begins now. May this book serve as a compass, guiding you through the tempests to a harbor of peace and success. Your story is not one of mere survival but a beacon for all who navigate the stormy seas of life. Let us embark on this journey together, with courage, determination, and the unwavering belief in our capacity to transcend the trials we face.

Introduction

I'll be honest with you from the start—the memories I'm about to share are not easy. They are raw, unfiltered, and etched into the deepest recesses of my being. They speak of a childhood marred by circumstances that no child should ever have to face. But they also reveal a fire within me; a relentless spirit that refused to be extinguished.

It all began with a blur—a blur of sirens and flashing lights; a blur of fear and confusion. I was just a wide-eyed seven-year-old when I raced down the stairs of our cramped apartment in Columbus, Georgia. My heart pounded in my chest as I caught sight of my mother being carried away on a stretcher by paramedics. At that moment, my world shifted, teetering on the precipice of an uncertain future.

Left in the wake of that fateful day were my younger brother and me; two innocent souls thrust into a turbulent and unpredictable existence within the foster care system. The very notion of "home" became an elusive concept, as we were shuttled from one place to another, our lives entangled in a web of temporary shelters, unfamiliar faces, and fleeting moments of stability.

But let me be clear—this journey was not one paved with rose petals and silver linings. No, it was a journey marked by unimaginable abuse, neglect, and the haunting specter of trauma. Nights were spent clutching onto fragments of hope, praying for a glimmer of light to pierce through the darkness that threatened to consume us.

Yet, amidst the chaos and confusion, a fire burned within my soul. It burned with a fervor that refused to be extinguished; a determination to rise above the circumstances that sought to define me. Dreams became my sanctuary—a refuge from the pain, a beacon of possibility in a world that seemed determined to keep me down.

And so, I clung to those dreams with every fiber of my being. They became my compass, guiding me through the labyrinth of foster homes, the ever-changing faces of caregivers, and the constant ache for a sense of belonging. They were my lifeline, reminding me that there was more to my story than the scars I carried.

As I reflect on the struggles of foster care, I am compelled to shine a light on the harsh realities faced by those who grow up within the system and eventually age out of it. And, before we delve further, it is important to acknowledge the facts. According to recent statistics, the average number of children in the foster care system in the United States hovers around 391,000. Of those children, only about 28% are adopted before aging out of the system.[1] That leaves hundreds of thousands of children, in our own country, who are traveling through the revolving door of foster care homes. When we look at education, only 50% of children in foster care graduate from high school, and less than 10% obtain a higher degree.[2] Now consider housing. At least 50% of the homeless population nationwide has spent time in foster care.[3] This number represents a significant portion of our society grappling with a journey fraught with challenges and obstacles that many cannot fathom. In writing this memoir, my intention is not only to share my personal story but also to bring attention to the broader societal issues that surround foster care.

Growing up in foster care means constantly adapting to new environments, facing uncertainty, and grappling with a lack of stability. It is a rollercoaster ride of emotions, as each transition brings a mix of hope and fear. The bonds formed with caregivers are often fleeting, leaving a profound sense of loss and longing for a place to call home.

Moreover, the foster care system is far from perfect. It is riddled with flaws, from overcrowded group homes to overwhelmed caseworkers. The consequences of these shortcomings are felt by the children who are caught in the system's grip. They endure the consequences of underfunding, lack of resources, and a shortage of qualified caregivers.

---

1 U.S. Department of Health and Human Services, Administration for Children and Families, Administration on Children, Youth and Families, Children's Bureau. "AFCARS Report No. 29: Preliminary FY 2021 Estimates as of June 28, 2022." 2022.
2 National Foster Youth Institute. "Higher Education."
3 National Foster Youth Institute. "Homelessness." https://nfyi.org/issues/homelessness/.

Through my experiences, I hope to humanize those statistics and shed light on the individual stories that often go unheard. I intend to give a voice to those who have been silenced by circumstances beyond their control. By haring my journey, I aim to spark empathy and understanding in the hearts of readers, fostering a greater sense of compassion and urgency for reform.

In delving into the struggles of foster care, it is crucial to confront the harsh realities head-on. It is a system that demands our attention, as it shapes the lives of countless children who deserve stability, love, and a chance to thrive. By shining a light on these issues, we can work towards creating positive change and ensuring a brighter future for those who come after us.

The struggles of foster care are not to be taken lightly. They are battles fought against the odds, and they demand our attention and empathy. Through this memoir, I aim to shed light on the realities of growing up in foster care and aging out of it. It is my sincerest hope that by sharing my journey, we can foster a greater understanding and work towards creating a more compassionate and supportive foster care system for future generations. After reading this, I hope that current foster youth can take my story and apply it to their own, so that they can develop the same mental toughness, resilience, and "never give up" mindset to accomplish their goals and dreams. As you approach the end of this book, I want you to give up the "I am a victim" mentality and instead embrace a "bend but don't break" mindset. As a foster youth, you are going to face disappointment, pain, sadness, depression, and anxiety, but I also know that with the right support system and mindset, you will find strength, determination, happiness, and most importantly, success. You can be confident knowing that whether you emancipate out of the system, go back to live with biological family, or get adopted, that you are in charge of your life, and if you make good choices, you will have good outcomes. You can be whatever you want to be, whether you want to pursue an MBA at a top university, go to trade school and be an HVAC technician, or join the military and serve your country. It is your life and it's time to start making positive decisions here in the present that will lay the foundation for a successful future.

The Heart of Columbus

Peabody Apartments: a cluster of worn low-rise buildings, loomed ahead, casting a dreary shadow over our lives. It was the place we called home after leaving Birmingham, Alabama, the city of my birth. At that time, it was just my mother, my baby brother Preston, and me, not even three years old yet. Unbeknownst to me, my father was already gone, and I would never have the chance to meet him. The apartments were a cacophony of noise, with voices and music echoing between the cramped walls. Most families that resided there seemed broken or struggling, much like our own.

Our modest two-bedroom unit was nestled towards the back of the complex. From our kitchen window, I would watch the daily bustle unfold at the nearby health department. Preston, as a toddler, would sit on the front steps, captivated by the people and routines he observed each day. The journey to the corner

corner grocery store was no small feat for us kids—a nearly two-mile walk in each direction. I can still vividly recall the image of my mom pushing Preston in a stroller while I toddled alongside, navigating the bustling streets under the scorching sun.

Every trip took a toll on my mother. Even at such a tender age, I could see how the physical exertion drained her energy. Her face would flush beet-red and splotchy; her chest heaving as she struggled to catch her breath upon our return. Sometimes, she would collapse into bed for hours, exhausted. I didn't fully comprehend then why walking was so arduous for her, but I knew that her health issues made everyday tasks a struggle.

Wherever we went, people's eyes seemed to follow us—with curiosity, confusion, or outright disapproval. We must have appeared as an unconventional sight, our little mixed-race family. My brother and I, with our light brown skin and hair, felt exposed under the weight of those judgmental gazes. My mom would steel her expression, urging us to keep moving, to ignore the looks as best we could.

Our lives relied on donated clothes and food stamps, as my mother's health conditions prevented her from working. She battled obesity, asthma, high blood pressure, and depression, grappling with the physical and emotional symptoms that accompanied those challenges. Amidst our hardships, the church provided solace. Most Sundays, members of the congregation would pick us up, and I cherished those moments—being surrounded by music and the warmth of other children.

As my mother's health continued to deteriorate, an increasing burden fell upon my young shoulders. I learned to cook basic meals on our gas stove, ensuring that Preston and I had something warm to eat. By the age of five, I had become an expert at giving my brother baths and getting him dressed for bed. My strength compensated for my mother's weaknesses, and her praises and pride in my abilities fueled my determination to persevere. I loved my mom. I knew she struggled, but she spent the energy she had trying to teach me how to find my place in the world. On the other hand, I was a terrible older brother. I loved Preston, but I didn't know how to connect with him, and generally resorted to either isolation or fighting.

Occasionally, my maternal grandmother would visit, but age hindered her ability to provide extensive support. Every now and then, my aunt would stop by with groceries, or Preston's father would visit and stay for a day or two. Yet, they were fleeting presences in my life, and I never established a close bond with them. By the time I entered kindergarten, financial hardships had become a familiar companion, even though I could only begin to fathom how they would shape my future.

Life settled into a predictable pattern of normality. While my brother, who was still too young for school, staying home with my mother, I embarked on the short journey down the street to attend school. Each morning, I would hop onto the school bus, finding a seat amidst the chatter of other children. However, forging friendships didn't come easily to me during those early years. Instead, I learned to keep to myself, observing the interactions around me from a comfortable distance.

As the bus rattled along, I would gaze out the window, lost in my own thoughts. The passing scenery became a backdrop to my musings; a silent companion in my solitary world. I watched as familiar landmarks and familiar faces blended together, each day feeling like a repetition of the one before. The routine provided a sense of stability, but it also reinforced my tendency to retreat into my own thoughts.

Once at school, I would navigate the hallways with a quiet determination. The classroom became my refuge, a haven where I could immerse myself in books and knowledge. I found solace in the pages of stories, living vicariously through the characters who inhabited imaginary worlds. While other children formed bonds and engaged in playful banter, I remained on the outskirts, content in my own realm of imagination. I enjoyed learning, and quickly excelled in every area of academics. However, this would sometimes become a barrier, and I would act out in class out of boredom. The teachers were nice enough and understanding, but I didn't feel like anyone actually understood what life for me or my family was.

As the days turned into weeks and then into months, solitude became a familiar companion. I grew accustomed to the quiet moments spent with my thoughts, finding comfort in the stillness within myself. While my peers formed friendships and engaged in playful activities, I developed a resilience that stemmed from self-reliance. I learned to rely on my own inner strength and creativity, finding fulfillment in solitary pursuits.

Though the lack of friendships was sometimes a source of longing, I recognized the value in my ability to be self-sufficient. The hours spent in introspection allowed me to cultivate a deep sense of self-awareness and an appreciation for solitude. I discovered the power of my own mind; the capacity to create worlds and stories within myself.

Against All Odds

And so, in those early years, I became a silent observer; a student of life's complexities. While the world around me buzzed with social interactions and connections, I honed my ability to navigate the depths of my own thoughts. It was during this time that I learned the importance of self-discovery and the art of finding solace within oneself.

Love and Loss in Peabody Apartments

I was seven-years-old when my brother shook me awake frantically. A quick glance out my upstairs window revealed an ambulance and firetruck outside the apartment. When I ran down the stairs, my mother was being rolled out on a stretcher, and there was a patch of dark-stained blood on the carpet. The sight sent a chill down my spine, a stark reminder that life was fragile and unpredictable. Panic gripped my young heart as I realized the severity of the situation.

I wouldn't know until later, but my mother had been able to call 911 before she lost consciousness from a heart attack. In that moment, she fought for her life, clinging to the hope that help would arrive in time. I stood there, frozen, as the paramedics worked swiftly to stabilize her fragile state. The urgency in their movements was palpable, and the sound of sirens pierced through the air, creating a cacophony of turmoil.

I was in shock, completely unsure how to respond. A police officer came over to comfort me; his voice filled with a mix of concern and compassion. He reassured me that they had called my grandmother, who would take care of us while my mom was in the hospital. But in my young mind, the gravity of the situation was lost. I had no idea that when they loaded my mother into the back of the ambulance, it would be the last time I saw her. I did not even say goodbye.

My brother and I were quickly shuffled to my grandmother's house, seeking solace in the familiarity of her presence. The journey to her home felt long and surreal, as if time itself had slowed down. The weight of the unknown hung heavy in the air, and the silence inside the car was suffocating. We clung to each other, seeking comfort and reassurance in the midst of the chaos that had abruptly entered our lives.

For the next few days, my aunt and uncle took on the responsibility of picking me up and taking me to school. But the truth about my mother's condition remained shrouded in secrecy. No one really told me anything, leaving me in a state of confusion and uncertainty. Days passed in a blur of school, car rides, meals, and tossing and turning to sleep. I continued to navigate the mundane routine all the while carrying an invisible burden that weighed heavily on my young shoulders. I remember asking questions about my mother, but I was not taken to see her in the hospital, and no one could really answer my questions, so I stopped asking.

Finally, in the middle of a seemingly ordinary first-grade school day, I was called into the guidance counselor's office. The room felt suffocatingly small, and the air was thick with a somber heaviness. My uncle was there, his brow furrowed and matter of fact. It was in that moment that he delivered the devastating news - my mother had passed away.

Again, I simply sat in shock, the words hanging in the air, refusing to register in my young mind. I had no knowledge or experience with death, and the concept felt foreign and incomprehensible. I didn't cry. I couldn't cry. My emotions were locked away, buried beneath layers of confusion and disbelief. My uncle checked me out of school and drove me back to my grandmother's house where funeral arrangements were being made.

The days leading up to the funeral passed in a blur. Time seemed to warp, leaving me in a perpetual state of disorientation. My brother and I became specters; silent figures observing the fragmented remnants of a shattered family. We were the unfortunate byproducts of my mother's life, caught in a web of sorrow and uncertainty. I didn't go to school during this time, as the weight of grief and the logistical challenges overwhelmed our fragmented family. I had only seen my extended family a handful of times, so it felt like I was living among strangers. And they didn't seem to care much for my brother or me. We were simply there, an added burden to an already stressful grown-up situation.

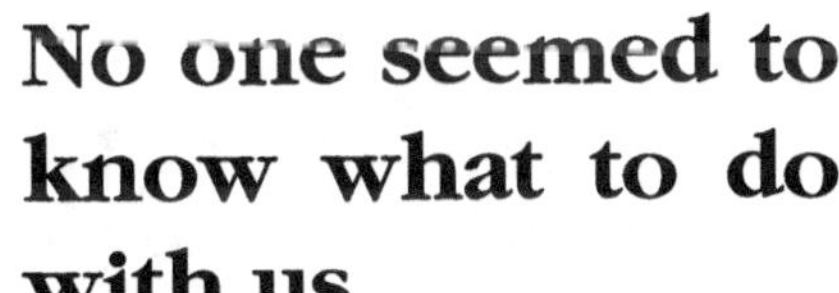

No one seemed to know what to do with us.

Finally, when the time came for the funeral, remember family members urging me to look at my mother in the casket. I just couldn't bring myself to do it. The thought of seeing her lifeless body, void of the vibrant spirit I had known, was too much to bear. In hindsight, I think I was completely unable to process what had happened, much less the reality of death. Hell, I was only seven. So, I made it through the funeral by staring blankly at the floor, the walls, anywhere but at my mother's body or the casket. I did not say goodbye or touch her one last time, as my grandmother encouraged. Some part of me held out hope that she may suddenly come alive again, sparing me from accepting this new grim reality.

The drive to the cemetery passed in a daze. The world outside the car window blurred into a tapestry of muted colors and indistinguishable shapes. As we stood around the grave after the burial ceremony, I remained silent and dry-eyed. I was still unable to grasp the finality of my mother's death or comprehend a life without her in it. The weight of grief bore down on me; its presence a constant companion in the days and weeks that followed.

In the aftermath of my mother's passing, I found myself navigating unfamiliar territory, trying to make sense of a world that had been irrevocably altered. However, grief has a way of numbing the senses, leaving one in a state of detachment. Instead of openly expressing my sadness, it manifested in my withdrawal from the world. I became an observer, moving through the motions of everyday life with a heavy heart and a sense of profound loss.

We stayed with my grandmother for about a month, seeking solace within the confines of her home. It was a space that held memories of my mother and

Poverty and Loss

being there provided a small measure of comfort. But as the days turned into weeks, it became evident that my grandmother, despite her best intentions, was ill-equipped to care for two young boys. Her home, nestled within a retirement community, was not conducive to the energy and needs of children. The realization dawned upon our extended family that we needed a more suitable environment.

And so, it was decided that my brother and I would embark on yet another transition; a journey to a new place that would become our temporary refuge. Little did I know that this would mark the beginning of a series of painful experiences that would test the limits of my young spirit.

The future held more pain than any child should have to endure, but at that moment, all I knew was that I was leaving behind the familiar comfort of my grandmother's home. The weight of loss and loneliness settled within me; a constant reminder of the void left by my mother's absence.

As we bid farewell to my grandmother, a bittersweet mixture of gratitude and sadness accompanied us on our journey. I clung to the memories of my mother, holding onto them like fragile treasures, afraid of forgetting the sound of her laughter or the warmth of her embrace.

Against All Odds

Through it all, I existed in a state of numbness, the tears refusing to flow, as if held captive by the weight of my grief. My young heart yearned for the solace that tears bring; the release that comes with acknowledging pain. But grief is a complex journey, and each individual traverses it in their own time.

Looking back, those early experiences of love and loss within the confines of Peabody Apartments shaped the person I would become. They taught me the fragility of life, the depths of grief, and the strength that can emerge from the ashes of pain. And though the road ahead seemed daunting, I would come to realize that even in the face of unimaginable adversity, love has the power to heal, to mend the broken pieces, and to illuminate the path forward.

The Darkest Days

My brother and I went to live with our aunt and uncle in a last-ditch effort to spare our grieving grandmother the burden of raising two young boys alone. Before my mother's passing, I hardly knew our extended family. Although my aunt would drop by occasionally to help my mom, she rarely paid attention to me, and I retreated back to my own world. So, when they announced that we were moving in with them, I had no clue whether it was a blessing or a curse. Besides, I was a seven-year-old boy who had just lost his mother. Nobody asked me for my opinion or where I wanted to go, but even if they had, I doubt I could have comprehended anything at that time.

One month after my mother's funeral, my brother and I packed our precious belongings into small bags and climbed into the car with our uncle. We moved into a tiny three-bedroom house with our aunt, who was pregnant at the time, her husband, and three cousins, all of whom were under the age of six. The house felt crowded, the walls closing in on us as we tried to navigate this new, unsettling chapter of our lives.

It was a time of transition for my aunt and uncle. They had both left their military careers behind and were trying to make ends meet with odd jobs. My petite, brunette-haired aunt sold insurance at Aflac while my towering, 6'2" uncle delivered pizzas for Dominos. My uncle's heavy drinking habit cast a dark cloud over the household, and as far as I observed, everyone was scared of him. His unpredictable temper created an atmosphere of fear and tension, leaving us constantly on edge.

My aunt was white, and my uncle was Vietnamese, and it didn't take long for us to realize that our skin color didn't sit well with them. They made it clear that my brother and I were a burden and an inconvenience. Whenever they had guests over, we were ordered to stay in our room and keep quiet, as if our presence was a stain on their carefully curated image. They were ashamed of us, as if we were responsible for our own existence and the circumstances that led us to their doorstep.

The abuse started off subtly at first. During mealtimes, my cousins would enjoy take-out or other tasty meals, while my brother and I were handed bologna sandwiches or hot dogs. It wasn't enough to satisfy our growing hunger, and we were constantly left feeling deprived. When we mustered the courage to ask why we couldn't have the same food as our cousins, they would dismissively tell us, "Well, you're not my kid." This disparity extended beyond meals to toys, clothes, and school supplies. My brother and I received nothing, and anything we had when we moved in was promptly taken away or given to my cousins. We were not allowed to play with toys and rarely given the opportunity to interact with our cousins, further isolating us in this unfamiliar environment.

But it wasn't just the lack of basic necessities that hurt us. As time went on, the abuse escalated, leaving scars on our young hearts and minds. They would scream at us, hurling racial slurs and demeaning insults, stripping away our sense of self-worth. If it wasn't a school day, the expectation was that I would stand in the corner of my room facing the wall, without bathroom breaks or food. It was a form of psychological torment; a constant reminder of my supposed worthlessness. If my uncle arrived home and found me not standing in the corner, he would forcefully drag me out into the tiled foyer of the house, subjecting me to a cruel punishment. He would make me stand on my head, with my feet leaning against the wall and my hands behind my back. The pain and discomfort were excruciating, and if I eventually lost my balance and fell, he would ruthlessly beat me with a weightlifting belt;

each strike leaving a physical and emotional imprint on my fragile spirit.

The cruelty extended beyond the confines of the house. My uncle had a Rottweiler that he would sic on my brother and me in the backyard. The dog would chase us relentlessly; its snarls and barks echoing in our ears as we ran for our lives. The fear of being bitten was constant; a threat that loomed over us with each passing day.

Whenever I found myself in trouble at school or home, my uncle's sadistic punishments knew no bounds. He would make me stand outside in the scorching Georgia sun; my face pressed against the wooden fence, and my hands behind my back. Time seemed to stretch endlessly as I endured the sweltering heat and the isolation; my pleas for mercy falling on deaf ears. He would mockingly tell me, "Since you want to act like a criminal, you're going to be treated like one." The small sip of water I received was barely enough to quench my thirst, and if I dared to ask for more, it invited further beatings and humiliation.

Amid the daily torment, I was also burdened with responsibilities beyond my years. One of my assigned tasks was to mow the yard. At seven-years-old, I could barely muster the strength to pull the choke cord and start the mower. The weight of the machine felt overwhelming, and I struggled to navigate the uneven terrain of the yard. Each time I faltered or asked for help, I would be met with a barrage of insults and berating remarks. There was no kindness or understanding for my young age and limited capabilities. Instead, I was forced to spend hours under the scorching sun, pushing the heavy mower through the grass; my parched throat crying out for relief. Yet, my aunt and uncle seemed oblivious to the physical strain and emotional toll it took on me. To them, I was just a mere child; easily dismissed and disregarded.

Life had been tough for me ever since my mother's death and the move to a new home, and it reflected in my personality. I was struggling to adjust to my new surroundings and make friends at school. Even though my grades were still good, a wave of anger grew inside me that I couldn't control. As the days turned into weeks and the weeks into months, the darkness that enveloped my life only intensified. The abuse and neglect from my aunt and uncle were relentless, wearing down my spirit with each passing day. The weight of my mother's absence and the burden of my new living situation pressed heavily upon my young shoulders. I felt trapped in a world that offered me no solace; no respite from the pain.

An incident with my classmate was the breaking point; the culmination of all the anger and frustration that had been building inside me. It was a seemingly insignificant dispute, but in that moment, it became a symbol of all the injustice and maltreatment I had endured. As my classmate's words cut through the air, mocking and belittling me, something within me snapped.

Blinded by rage and fueled by the desire to assert myself, I lunged at my classmate, my small fists swinging wildly. The classroom erupted into chaos as the teacher and other students struggled to separate us. The fight was quickly broken up, but the damage had been done. The consequences of my actions were swift and severe.

I was immediately sent to the principal's office; my heart pounding with a mixture of fear and defiance. As expected, the principal called my uncle to tell him what had happened, and I panicked. I knew the consequences would be far beyond my control. I went through the rest of the school day in slow motion, dreading what would happen next.

As I stepped off the bus, I raced up the steps and opened the screen door, not realizing that my uncle was right behind me. The door slammed shut in his face, and before I could even turn around, his hands were on me, and he was screaming at me. He picked me up and began choking me. Eventually, I blacked out, and when I came to, I was lying on the floor, gasping for air. My uncle was still screaming at me, telling me to get up. I stumbled to my feet, my heart pounding in my chest, and ran to my room as fast as I could.

Survival

After that first choking incident, it was as if a dam had burst. The physical abuse that had always been lurking beneath the surface was now out in the open, and there was no escaping it. The cramped house that had never felt safe before was now a veritable house of horrors.

I dreaded coming home from school every day. The walk back from the school bus felt like a death march, and there were times when I seriously thought that I might not make it out alive. My aunt and uncle seemed to take pleasure in beating me with belts and hitting me with anything they could get their hands on - the TV remote, the weightlifting belt, or their bare hands. It always got worse when my uncle had been drinking. And when I tried to take a bath, my uncle would try to drown me in the tub, just for fun.

One particular evening, my uncle decided to take my brother and me along to visit one of his coworkers.

Against All Odds

As usual, we found ourselves relegated to the corners of the room, feeling somewhat out of place amidst the unfamiliar faces. Eventually, fatigue caught up with us, and we found solace in the guest bedroom, drifting off to sleep.

However, our peaceful slumber was abruptly interrupted around midnight. My uncle woke us up and hurriedly ushered us into his car. The purpose of our late-night excursion remained a mystery as we embarked on a drive that was filled with an air of tension and uncertainty.

After what felt like an eternity, we arrived at a serene lake, its surface glistening under the moonlight. Without uttering a single word, my uncle abruptly left us there, standing at the water's edge. It was then that we realized we were expected to swim, despite neither my brother nor I having any swimming skills.

Fear gripped us as we struggled in the water, desperately trying to stay afloat and gasping for air. The situation seemed dire, and for a moment, we felt overwhelmed and afraid for our lives. However, by some stroke of luck, we managed to reach the safety of the shore.

After what seemed like an eternity, my uncle returned, saying nothing. We climbed back into the car; our minds filled with confusion and unanswered questions. The drive back to his coworker's house was shrouded in silence, leaving us grappling with the bewildering experience we had just endured.

In the aftermath of that night, the incident remained unspoken between us, leaving a lingering sense of betrayal and mistrust.

It became increasingly evident that my uncle's marriage to my aunt was under immense strain. After about three months of residing in their house, my brother and I found ourselves moving in with my uncle's parents. Unfortunately, the new living arrangements were even more cramped than before, and we were assigned to sleep in the laundry room.

During this time, my aunt's presence in the house became sporadic, and we saw less of her compared to earlier. On the other hand, my uncle's mother, a kind-hearted Vietnamese woman we affectionately called "Grandma," did her best to intervene whenever possible, offering solace and support. She would prepare meals for us, ensuring we were nourished and cared for alongside the rest of the family. However, despite her efforts, she couldn't shield us from every hardship that unfolded.

One night, my brother was taking a bath, accompanied

by two of my cousins, when my uncle barged into the bathroom unannounced. He swiftly ordered his own children to leave, firmly shutting and locking the door behind them. The sounds that followed were unimaginable.

My brother's desperate screams for help and the chilling gasps for air pierced through the closed door, engulfing us in a horrifying symphony of terror. It was clear that my uncle was attempting to drown him; his rage spiraling out of control. In that moment of sheer chaos, it was my "grandma," the gentle Vietnamese lady, who summoned an extraordinary reserve of courage.

With unyielding determination, she broke down the door, launching herself onto my uncle's back and forcibly pulling him away from my brother. The scene that awaited us inside the bathroom was a haunting tableau of bloodshed. My brother's head had been grievously injured; his skin sliced open by the unforgiving edge of the bathtub. Without hesitation, my uncle's mother swiftly rushed him to the hospital; her love and concern propelling her into action.

Despite nearly killing my brother, the abuse continued. My body was constantly covered in scars and bruises. My uncle's cruelty knew no bounds, and it was always accompanied by vile, racist comments that cut me to the core. Survival mode became my default state of being. I would hide food when I could, and attending school felt like a relief. I dreaded summer vacation when I would have to be stuck at the house. Every day brought with it a fresh round of beatings and tortuous punishments. There were times when the abuse was so severe that my uncle would keep me home from school, afraid that someone would ask questions about my cuts and bruises.

I felt powerless to stop the abuse. I was trapped in a living nightmare, with no end in sight. All I could do was endure the pain and pray for a way out. But as the days turned into weeks, and the weeks turned into months, it became clear that there was no escape.

I was stuck in this hellish existence, with no hope of rescue.

So, when they let me leave for school with a black eye, I was surprised. Maybe they were too busy taking care of their own kids to remember to hide the evidence. But that oversight turned out to be my saving grace.

Against All Odds

As I walked to my classroom, my teacher pulled me aside and discreetly asked what had happened to my face. I told her the truth: I had fought with my uncle, and he had hit me. She immediately took me to the principal's office, where they asked me if I had any other bruises. I hesitated for a moment, unsure if I should expose my reality to the world. But then I realized that I had nothing left to lose.

I slowly took off my clothes, revealing a patchwork of bruises and scars across my entire body. The adults in the room were visibly shocked by what they saw. They called the police and Child Protective Services, and I went through a series of interviews, answering questions in the hopes that I would never have to go back to that house. This incident, combined with my brother's suspicious visit to the emergency room, made it evident that we were not in a safe home.

I'm not entirely sure what the procedures were, but I remember feeling a glimmer of hope for the first time in a long time. Although I had to go home after school that day, the abuse had miraculously stopped. Within a month, my uncle sat my brother and me down and explained that we would no longer be living with them.

It was a fresh start, a chance to escape the nightmare that had been my life for so long. And although the road ahead was uncertain, I knew that I had been given a second chance - and this time, I wasn't going to let anyone take it away from me.

Chapter 3: Entering the Foster Care System

Lost and Alone at Nine

The morning when our first caseworker arrived remains etched in my memory as a surreal experience. Wordlessly, my brother and I hurriedly packed our meager belongings into trash bags as the sun gradually arose outside our window. We didn't spare a glance back at the house that had been our confining prison as we climbed into the caseworker's car. A heady mix of nervousness and excitement overwhelmed me at that moment. We were finally escaping, but I had no idea what awaited us beyond those car doors. I was now nine-years-old and had already lived enough for a lifetime.

The caseworker, with a gentle tone, explained that we were being removed from our aunt and uncle's home due to mistreatment. We were to enter the foster care system, although my understanding of what that truly entailed was vague at best. In those bewildering moments, all I knew for certain was that we would no longer have to endure the torment of living with our abusive guardians. And for now, that was enough. I remember asking the case worker if my brother and I would ever have to go back to live with my aunt and uncle, and she shook her head and said that it was highly unlikely since we had been so severely abused. I breathed a sigh of relief.

After a short drive, we arrived at our new home. Our new foster parents, a middle-aged couple, welcomed us inside. On the surface, they seemed amiable enough, but their tired smiles and vacant eyes betrayed a lack of genuine warmth or concern for us. We were not embraced as new members of a family; rather, we were viewed as sources of additional income.

The caseworker placed my brother and me together in our first foster home. It took us some time to adjust and recover from the trauma we had experienced. My brother and I shared a small room in the new house, but we didn't talk very much. I don't think either of us knew how to process what had happened in the past year, and while we had each other's backs, we functioned fairly independently of each other. We had to learn to destress and shift out of survival mode, trying to understand our new surroundings and what it meant to live in foster care.

In the initial weeks that followed, my brother and I felt like spectators aimlessly drifting through the lives of these strangers. The couple tended to our basic needs but displayed no genuine interest in our well-being or aspirations. I now comprehend that this transactional relationship is all too common in foster care, where individuals open their homes to foster children primarily as a means of extended babysitting, devoid of any true desire to nurture.

I continued attending the same school, but the trauma inflicted by my aunt and uncle made it challenging to feel safe and secure anywhere. The memories of their abuse lingered, casting a shadow over my interactions with classmates and teachers. I struggled to trust others, always on guard for signs of impending harm. Despite my best efforts to blend in, I carried the weight of my past with me; a burden that overshadowed my ability to fully engage in academic and social activities.

At school, my teachers and principals were incredibly supportive and apologetic about what had happened to us. They assured me that they were on our side and encouraged me to reach out to them if I ever needed help or someone to talk to. Their compassion and understanding provided a glimmer of hope amidst the darkness, reminding me that there were individuals who genuinely cared about my well-being.

Within the confines of our new foster home, the wounds of our past continued to haunt us. My brother and I grappled with a pervasive sense of instability and uncertainty. We yearned for stability and a sense of belonging, but it remained elusive. Our foster parents, preoccupied with their own lives and seemingly indifferent to our emotional needs, perpetuated a cycle of neglect.

I resorted to secretly taking food from the kitchen, hoarding it in my room—an instinctive response to the deprivation I had endured. Looking back, I recognize this coping mechanism as a trauma-induced reaction. However, my foster parents saw it merely as defiance and deception. Their punitive response further deepened my feelings of isolation and reinforced the belief that I was unworthy of care and nourishment.

Within six months, they concluded that my brother and I were more trouble than we were worth. With barely a word, they deposited us back at the doorstep of social services. The cycle began anew. Once again, we found ourselves in a state of uncertainty, shuttled from one temporary placement to another; our sense of stability shattered. Sadly, this became the reality of my life until I aged out of the system at eighteen.

Preston and I were also placed together in our second foster home. We had to switch schools, but only stayed for a few months before we were moved again. It became a revolving door of foster homes, and honestly, I don't think I can even remember all of them. My brother and I were split up after the first two foster homes, because the case worker struggled to find someone to keep both of us. We would still see each other on scheduled visits, but we didn't live together again for a while.

Each transition brought new faces, new rules, and a relentless sense of impermanence. It was a constant struggle to adapt; to find a semblance of normalcy amid the ever-changing landscape of foster care. The system meant to protect us often felt like a revolving door, where we were merely passed from one set of caretakers to the next, without any real consideration for our well-being or long-term stability.

The Revolving Door

With each new placement, I learned to adapt more quickly; to navigate the intricacies of different households and the unique dynamics within them. Some foster families welcomed me with open arms, providing a temporary haven where I felt valued and cared for. Others, however, mirrored the transactional nature of our first foster home, leaving me feeling like an inconvenience rather than a whole human in need of love and support.

Amidst the turbulent currents of my life, education

emerged as a steadfast sanctuary—a realm that offered respite from the uncertainties that plagued my daily existence. Beyond its traditional role as a place of learning, school became a refuge where I could immerse myself in the world of books, ideas, and the pursuit of knowledge. Within the walls of the classroom, I discovered a sense of purpose and direction, a glimmer of hope that transcended the limitations imposed by my circumstances. Academically, I excelled. My problem quickly became boredom in the classroom, which resulted in my acting out. So, the cycle of calls home and unhappy foster parents continued, and I felt continually overlooked and misunderstood.

Teachers played an instrumental role in shaping my journey, not solely as educators but as compassionate mentors who recognized my untapped potential. They encouraged me to dream beyond the confines of my current reality, serving as beacons of inspiration and guidance. Understanding the disruption that had punctuated my education, they went above and beyond to bridge the gaps in my knowledge, offering additional support and personalized instruction to help me catch up and flourish academically.

Beyond the realm of academics, the school community became a source of stability and belonging. I formed connections with fellow classmates who, like me, carried their own burdens and bore the marks of their individual struggles. Together, we forged a support network—a chosen family that understood the intricate complexities of our lives. In sharing our experiences, we found comfort and strength, creating an environment where empathy and understanding flourished.

Yet, the transient nature of my living arrangements often necessitated changing foster homes and, consequently, switching schools. This constant upheaval transformed the idea of a stable school community into an elusive dream rather than an everyday reality. Gradually, I found myself withdrawing from forming deep connections and hesitating to cultivate new friendships, knowing that the impending upheaval of yet another move would sever those ties. The fear of transience overshadowed the potential joys of friendship, and I retreated into myself as a self-protective measure.

Nonetheless, the echoes of those fleeting connections and the support they offered remained etched in my heart. They served as reminders of the profound impact that stable relationships and a nurturing community can have on one's well-being. In the midst of the turbulence, I clung to the memories of the camaraderie and understanding I had experienced, reminding myself that, despite the transitory nature of my existence, the power of human connection can endure and shape lives in remarkable ways.

Sadly, the next several foster homes that my brother and

Against All Odds

I were placed in followed a painfully familiar script. We would be shuffled into a new home, only to be shuffled right back out within a matter of months when the foster parents deemed the "babysitting job" too tough to handle. It was as if we were temporary burdens, conveniently discarded when our presence became inconvenient.

Each time we were returned to social services by our foster parents, they would offer the same hollow words of explanation: "This just isn't working out." I wanted to scream in frustration, to tell them that, of course, it wasn't working out. They had never truly tried to care for us as people; they only saw us as sources of income; mere paychecks to cash. But I remained silent, my voice drowned out by a mix of anger, disappointment, and resignation as I numbly gathered my few belongings once again.

The exhausting cycle of continually adapting to new environments took a heavy toll on my brother and me. Every foster home had its own set of rules, expectations, and often, a revolving door of other foster kids cycling through. Just as I began to grow accustomed to a school and forge a few fragile friendships, we would be abruptly uprooted and forced to start all over again in a strange and unfamiliar place.

Entering the Foster Care System

By the time I reached fourth grade, the memories of each foster family began to blur together. I had lived in six, maybe seven different foster homes by then, though honestly, I had lost count. Only two of them had been with my brother, the rest I had endured alone. They became meaningless blips on the radar of my life as my sense of permanence withered away. It seemed as though we would never find a real home with caring and loving parents.

Regardless of our placement, the foster homes all shared a common thread—an emotionally distant vibe that seemed to say, "We'll let you stay here, but don't expect anything more. Keep quiet, don't make trouble, and stay out of our way." I quickly learned that most foster parents didn't care about our well-being or personal growth; as long as the monthly check cleared, they were content.
With each passing day, my sense of self-worth rapidly deteriorated. I felt like nothing more than a piece of luggage, constantly being dumped on doorstep after doorstep. The hopes I once held of finding a loving and nurturing family were fading fast, eroded by the harsh reality of multiple failed placements.

After enduring numerous disappointments in foster care, our caseworker recognized the urgent need to ensure that my brother and I remained together. It was at this point that we received news of our transfer to a group home facility called Hephzibah.

Against All Odds

Hephzibah House

Nestled amidst the tranquil landscapes of rural Georgia, Hephzibah sprawled across a vast expanse of 205 acres; its expansive homes thoughtfully designed to accommodate boys and girls across different age groups. Supervised by live-in house parents, who exuded an outward aura of kindness and good intentions, each house provided a nurturing environment for ten children.

After enduring six or seven transitions between foster homes, my brother Preston and I found ourselves at Hephzibah—a temporary refuge that would become our home for over a year, nearly two. I was merely a fourth grader, just ten-years-old at the time. Suitable placements for us were becoming scarce, and Hephzibah emerged as a solution to address this challenge.

The sprawling campus housed four cottages, each dedicated to a specific age group—small girls, teenage girls, small boys, and teenage boys. Thanks to financial support from various churches and sponsors, the facility boasted an array of activities that enriched our lives. We had access to football fields, basketball courts, four-wheelers, bicycles, and more. In the dining facility, our nutritional needs were met, and during special occasions like Christmas and birthdays, we were blessed with abundant gifts from sponsors. Moreover, we were fortunate enough to attend quality schools, with me even enrolled in a private institution, offering a glimmer of hope for a brighter future.

Compared to the austere foster homes that had marked our tumultuous journey, Hephzibah felt like a sanctuary—a place where the wounds of our past began to heal. Generous funding infused the facility with thoughtful gestures, such as birthday and holiday gifts, bringing moments of joy and normalcy to our lives. Additionally, I was fortunate enough to attend a nearby private school and engage in sports activities on the sprawling fields and courts; a stark departure from the constant upheaval that had come to define my existence.

For the first time in what seemed like an eternity, a glimmer of security and a sense of community began to emerge. Yet, the raw wounds of past abuse made it arduous for me to forge meaningful connections with the other boys in my house. My behavior, a reflection of the internal turmoil I grappled with, oscillated between brooding silence and uncontrollable bursts of rage. During moments of overwhelming emotions, the house parents would confine me to a small, windowless room in the basement for 24 hours, where I battled the inner demons that plagued me. In hindsight, I understand that they needed to place me separately from the other children, but that particular punishment was never very effective for me.

Hephzibah also employed a disciplinary system rooted in incentives, where privileges were earned through good behavior. However, despite consistently achieving high grades academically, my restless and disruptive demeanor in class often landed me in trouble. The cycle of punishment and isolation persisted, casting shadows over the supposedly nurturing environment that surrounded us.

My time at Hephzibah proved to be one of the more positive experiences I had within the foster care system. However, despite the overall positive environment, my problematic behavior eventually led to my departure from the group home. My struggles in school and a lack of respect towards the house parents disrupted the harmony within the facility.

Hephzibah employed a level system of discipline, where higher levels granted more privileges. Unfortunately, my behavior and attitude led to a downward spiral, and I found myself confined to a special room in the basement— an austere wooden space with bars—for up to 24 hours. This disciplinary measure was meant to help me reflect on my actions and make positive changes.

After nearly two years of residing at Hephzibah, the house parents reluctantly sat me down to convey their decision. They acknowledged that my frequent outbursts and defiance indicated a lack of adjustment to the group home environment. It was a heart-wrenching moment as they explained that, once again, I would be uprooted and placed back into the foster care system. This news shattered the tenuous sense of stability I had managed to establish, and overwhelming emotions of anger and profound loneliness enveloped me.

As my hopes for a lasting sense of belonging were abruptly shattered once more, I grappled with the harsh reality of the foster care system. The constant upheaval and uncertainty made it difficult to trust and form meaningful connections. Despite the setback, I held onto the belief that someday I would find a place where I truly belonged, where my past wouldn't define my future.

Chapter 4: Glimmers of Hope

The Cycle Continues

After being removed from Hephzibah, my brother and I found ourselves placed with a single older woman named Ms. Tremble. Her name seemed to perfectly match the atmosphere of her home, which I despised. This wasn't my first time being placed with her, and I wasn't thrilled about going back. From the moment I stepped foot into her house, I knew it was going to be a difficult journey.

Ms. Tremble's home was strict, and some might even say abusive. The rules and expectations were rigid, leaving little room for individuality or emotional expression. To earn something as simple as a pillow or a blanket, you had to prove your obedience and good behavior for a week or two. It was disheartening to realize that even basic necessities were conditional in this environment. The pattern was always the same — if you wanted comfort, you had to endure a long period of impeccable behavior. The constant feeling of having to earn every little thing grated on my nerves, and I couldn't stand it.

While my brother seemed to adjust relatively well to Ms. Tremble's home, I made up my mind to run away. After just two months, I reached a breaking point. I wanted to make a statement, assert my autonomy, and protest against the oppressive conditions I was subjected to. And so, I made my escape. It was a desperate act, driven by frustration and the desire for change.

My decision to run away had an immediate impact. Ms. Tremble promptly kicked me out of her home but decided to keep my brother in her care. It was a painful separation, yet I hoped that by taking this drastic step, I would draw attention to the injustices and difficulties I faced in that environment.

After being expelled from the Tremble household, I found myself back at the Muscogee County Emergency Shelter where I had sought refuge on a few previous occasions. Normally, the shelter offered temporary housing for transitioning youth for about 30 days, providing a temporary respite and stability. However, my stay turned out to be longer than expected, as the challenges of finding a suitable placement persisted.

The shelter was run by a compassionate couple, Ann and Eric Wyatt, whom I had grown familiar with during my previous visits. They not only served as caretakers at the shelter but also dedicated themselves to being therapeutic foster parents outside of its walls. Their commitment to providing a safe and nurturing environment for children in need was evident in everything they did.

During my time at the shelter, I witnessed firsthand the love and care Ann and Eric poured into the children they welcomed into their home. They had already taken in another child who required a higher level of care, demonstrating their unwavering dedication to supporting those who needed it most. Their presence in my life became a beacon of hope, reminding me that there were people who genuinely cared about my well-being and were willing to go the extra mile to make a difference.

When the time came for me to leave the shelter, Ann and Eric approached me with an unexpected offer. They extended an invitation for me to become part of their own family by offering me a place in their home in Columbus, Georgia. It was an opportunity I eagerly embraced, as the prospect of finding a stable and caring home felt like a long-awaited lifeline.

Living with the Wyatts proved to be an entirely different experience from anything I had encountered before. From the moment I entered their home, they exuded a parental aura, genuinely caring for me and actively engaging with me in a way that was foreign yet comforting. Their level of involvement and genuine concern for my well-being was something entirely new and transformative in my life.

As we began to develop a deeper connection, the Wyatts broached the subject of me officially joining their family. Without hesitation, I wholeheartedly agreed, recognizing that this was an opportunity to belong to a family that would provide the love, support, and stability I had always yearned for. For nearly two years, I lived with them, and during that time, I experienced what it truly meant to be part of a nurturing and caring family.

The Wyatts' household was built on a strong religious foundation, and they placed great emphasis on maintaining good health, both physically and emotionally. They were deeply involved in church activities, and their house, nestled in a pleasant neighborhood, boasted a backyard swimming pool that became a hub of joyful moments and cherished memories. It felt like a normal home; a place where I could experience the simple joys of childhood and find solace in a stable environment.

Throughout my stay, the Wyatts went above and beyond for me. They made sure to check in on me regularly, offering guidance and support. They helped me with homework, celebrated my achievements, and provided a nurturing environment where I could grow and thrive. Their love extended far beyond the basics of shelter and food; they showered me with care and affection in ways I had never experienced before. One notable example was during Christmas, where they spent a considerable amount of money on gifts; a gesture that touched my heart deeply. It was a testament to their commitment to making me feel cherished and valued as a member of their family.

What struck me most about my time with the Wyatts was their unwavering acceptance and inclusion. Ann and Eric, a Caucasian couple, never hesitated to have me by their side. They treated me as their own, embracing and celebrating our differences while fostering an environment of love and understanding. They allowed me to embrace my childhood, encouraging me to simply go out and play, to experience the joys of being a carefree kid.

In their home, I finally felt like I had a genuine set of parents who saw me for who I was and loved me unconditionally.

Against All Odds

The Wyatts became my refuge, my safe haven, and the only place where I truly felt like I had found my forever home. Their immense love, care, and dedication helped heal the wounds of my past, instilling in me a sense of hope and a belief that I deserved happiness and stability. I will forever be grateful for the time I spent with them, and the impact they had on my life will never fade. They showed me what family should feel like, and their unwavering support ignited a flame of resilience within me that continues to guide me on my journey.

Adopted and Abandoned

However, our lives took an unexpected turn when the caseworker delivered a surprising update. It turned out that there was a couple interested in adopting both Preston and me. I must admit that I wasn't initially thrilled about the prospect. I had grown to love the Wyatts deeply, and the thought of any change, even if it meant staying with my brother, didn't sit well with me. I had held onto the hope that the Wyatts themselves would adopt us or at least allow us to continue living together, as we had previously discussed. But this new opportunity seemed more permanent, and the Wyatts encouraged me to give it a chance.

Glimmers of Hope

Reluctantly, Preston and I were uprooted from our familiar surroundings and transported to a remote location to embark on a "trial" period with the prospective adoptive couple. We spent a week in this unfamiliar setting, which soon turned into months as the couple decided to extend the trial. However, over time, it became evident that the adoption process was not progressing as expected. I was in the seventh grade at the time, and being in the middle of nowhere with limited activities and distractions was far from ideal for me. I struggled with discipline and resented being told what to do by a couple in their mid-fifties who had no understanding of the life I had lived. The stark contrast between their expectations and my own experiences bred a sense of frustration and detachment.

Moreover, deep within me simmered a sense of anger and grief at having been removed from the Wyatts' loving home. It was difficult to let go of the stability and warmth I established there, and that resentment colored my view of this new situation. As a result, the revolving door of transitions resumed, and Preston and I were once again sent to different homes, further disrupting our sense of stability, and leaving us feeling adrift in a sea of uncertainty.

These series of transitions were challenging for both Preston and me. We longed for a place where we could find lasting stability and a sense of belonging. The constant upheaval took a toll on our emotional well-being and made it difficult to form lasting connections or trust in the system that seemed to shuffle us around without much consideration for our needs and desires.

The Pain of Starting Over

My experience in the foster care system took a sharp downturn as I navigated through a series of challenging placements following the attempted adoption. The stability and sense of belonging I had briefly glimpsed were swiftly replaced by a sense of uncertainty and disappointment.

First, I was sent to live with an elderly woman. From the moment I arrived, it became clear that this foster home was not the right fit for me. The woman lacked understanding and patience, and I felt a deep sense of discomfort and unhappiness during my time there. The environment was unfamiliar and unwelcoming, and it was evident that the woman did not possess the necessary knowledge or resources to provide the support I needed. Although I was grateful that this placement did not last long, the experience left a lasting impact on my well-being.

Glimmers of Hope

Preston's foster parent was willing to take me in as well. While my brother had experienced intermittent stays with her during his elementary school years prior to our time at Hephzibah, I had only stayed with her once before. Unfortunately, that previous stay had not ended well, as I had succumbed to a fit of anger and impulsively hurled something at her. This time, however, I was determined to make it work. I yearned to be by my brother's side, and it was evident that he felt a sense of comfort and security with this woman. I hoped that her kindness and acceptance of my brother would extend to me as well.

Despite my initial optimism, I found myself grappling to adapt to the new environment. While my brother's placement resulted in adoption, I remained in their home, but the sense of belonging eluded me. I felt disconnected, like an outsider in my supposed "home." Unwanted and unvalued, I sensed an underlying discomfort that permeated our interactions.

The foster parent, though undoubtedly well-intentioned, exhibited a strict and demanding demeanor that clashed with my temperament. The rules and expectations she set forth felt overwhelming, and I struggled to meet her standards. As time went on, it became increasingly apparent that I was not meeting her expectations, and I fell short of the mark in her eyes.

Against All Odds

The strain between us grew more pronounced with each passing day, and the tension eventually reached its breaking point. The foster parent made the difficult decision to ask me to leave. The feelings of rejection and inadequacy intensified, as I faced the reality of being uprooted once again. It was a devastating blow, as I had hoped desperately to find stability and acceptance within the confines of my brother's adoptive home.

This experience left me with mixed emotions. While I understood the complexities of the situation and the foster parent's decision to prioritize my brother's well-being, I couldn't help but feel a profound sense of longing for a place where I truly belonged. The brief taste of family life and the prospect of a permanent home had been tantalizingly close, only to slip through my grasp once more.

The pain of this setback lingered, and it was challenging to reconcile the disappointment with my ongoing search for a loving and stable family. I carried a heaviness in my heart as I faced the uncertainty of what lay ahead. Yet, within that pain, there remained a glimmer of hope—a determination to keep pushing forward, to continue seeking the place where I could find genuine acceptance and belonging.

Then, for almost two years, I lived with Edward

and Emma Stokes. They were an older couple—in their sixties—but they created a nurturing family environment. Edward had retired from the military, and Emma made homemade meals every night. It was a very grounding, stable time. I met their relatives, took trips with them, and they provided for me as if I was their own. Edward told me stories about his placements in the military, which opened my eyes to a career path that I had not been familiar with. They were involved in the church, so I attended alongside them. They also cared about my grades, who I hung out with, and how I spent my time. It was truly a family-centered atmosphere. Their daughter, Tonya, and her husband, Sammie, were also foster parents. Since they frequently had other kids in the house, I would spend Sunday afternoons with them, playing games, watching movies, and eating pizza. Gradually, I began spending more and more time with Tonya and Sammie, and they quickly became a huge part of my life and family. It was the first time I had seen extended family function together as a unit in a healthy and supportive way, and I cherished it. Even in my later years of foster care and college, I would go and visit Tonya and Sammie on occasion. They were younger, willing to have conversations, and were more relatable. To this day, they hold a big place in my heart, and I am deeply thankful for the ways they supported and provided for me.

Against All Odds

Unfortunately, I was assigned a new caseworker, who was not only new to being a caseworker but was very new to me. She didn't understand my patterns or behaviors, and removed me from the Stokes' home abruptly, without the Stokes' blessing. This was truly heartbreaking to me. I felt like I had found a family (and extended family) that I could be part of, and it was taken away with the click of a pen.

To Edward and Emma Stokes, although both of you are no longer here with us, I find myself reflecting on the countless ways you two shaped the person I am today. Though words can scarcely capture the depth of my gratitude, I want to try to express my thanks for the incredible role you both played in my life. You all were more than just foster parents; you both were beacons of wisdom, and role models of strength and integrity. The lessons you taught me about being a man with a strong work ethic and the importance of responsibility have become the foundation of my character. You showed me that hard work isn't just about what we accomplish, but it's about the person we become in the process. You were the main inspiration for me, wanting to serve my country and joining the Army. I never felt like I was the worst foster child in the world, but I've realized I was at times, hardheaded, stubborn, and thought I knew everything. You taught me that we all have two ears and one mouth so that we may listen twice as much as we talk. You all took me on trips and allowed me to experience life as part of your family. I will always be grateful to you both.

To Sammie and Tonya Burts, of all the foster parents that I ever came across, you two were hands down the most fun and nurturing. It was you two that gave me the nickname "Einstein," because I thought I knew everything and couldn't be told anything. You both epitomize patience, love, and compassion. You treat each other with the same grace, love, and empathy that I hope to show my wife and my children. A complete stranger could walk into your house and know that loving people live there. The contributions you both have made to foster youth like myself gives me hope for current foster youth. I hope that every child in the foster care system gets an opportunity to live in a home of peace, joy, and love the way I, and so many others, experienced at your home. Of the two dozen or so foster homes that I spent time in, I never truly felt at home like a did when I spent time with you all. I miss the pool parties, the intense games of spades, and pizza nights. Often times, I would forget that I was a foster kid when I stayed at your home. The way you both spoke life into me every time we interacted is what every foster youth needs. They need someone to believe in them, someone that truly cares about their well-being, and most importantly, is invested in our future. Whenever someone asks me what the perfect foster family was like, I would immediately think of you two.

The next foster home I entered during my tenth-grade year was a distressing experience. This particular foster family was a retired military household, consisting of a couple with two biological children and one additional foster care child, like myself. However, the dynamics within this home were marred by overt racism, causing them to treat us foster children vastly differently from their biological offspring.

From the moment I stepped foot into their home, it was made abundantly clear that we were not considered their real children. The constant reminders and dismissive attitude created an environment that left us feeling like unwelcome outsiders. It was a painful and disheartening realization that further compounded the challenges we already faced.

To add to the complexity of the situation, the father of the household manipulated me into taking on the responsibility of completing college courses on his behalf. This exploitative behavior played on my eagerness to be seen as valuable and capable, as I sought validation and acceptance within the confines of this foster family.

However, a critical turning point occurred when I

received an impressive A grade in one of the college courses I had taken for the father. I was sarcastic and had an attitude towards him, largely due to my frustrations at having been given this task without any benefit. They promptly called my case worker to report my behavior, and I was rather quickly removed from their home.

After being removed from the troubled foster home, my journey towards stability and independence continued. I found myself in a temporary placement; a short-term arrangement lasting only a week or two. This brief respite allowed me to regain some stability and gather my thoughts before moving on to the next phase of my life. Soon after, I was transferred to a transitional facility, specially designed for teenagers like me who were preparing to transition into independent living.

At the transitional facility, I joined three other individuals who were facing similar circumstances. Together, we embarked on an empowering journey, aiming to acquire the fundamental life skills and develop the necessary tools to thrive on our own. Over the course of a year and a half, the facility provided us with essential guidance and instruction on various aspects of independent living. We delved into subjects such as budgeting, employment preparation, cooking, and personal responsibility. The program was meticulously designed to equip us with the skills needed for a self-sufficient future.

Throughout this challenging period, I remained steadfast in managing my ADHD diagnosis. I had been diagnosed when I was young but had never truly received the attention or medicine to help manage it. But now, I have taken ownership and responsibility for my health.

One prevailing pattern I observed within the foster care system was the prevalence of homes where I felt like nothing more than an occupant. In these environments, there was minimal interaction or effort to build genuine relationships. Instead, it often seemed as though I was merely there to occupy a room, providing an additional source of income for the foster parents. The lack of genuine connection and effort to establish meaningful relationships further reinforced my sense of displacement and intensified my longing for a place where I would be valued and genuinely cared for.

Interestingly, it was recognized that I thrived best in foster homes without other children present. This understanding led to a decision to place me in environments that provided individual attention and support. It acknowledged the unique challenges I faced in forming relationships with other children within the foster care system. The transitional facility became the last true foster care home I ever stayed in, marking a significant milestone in my journey towards independence.

The transitional facility played a pivotal role in preparing me for the next steps in life. It provided a nurturing and supportive environment where I could learn and grow. Equipped with the life skills and knowledge imparted during my time there, I felt increasingly prepared to face the challenges that lay ahead. It instilled in me a sense of resilience, determination, and self-reliance.

As my time in the transitional facility drew to a close, a new chapter in my life beckoned—the pursuit of higher education. College became my aspiration, a path that promised not only academic growth but also a newfound sense of belonging and purpose. With the support and guidance, I had received, I felt ready to take on this new endeavor and forge a brighter future for myself.

Chapter 5: The Road to College

Senior Year

As my senior year began in November 2006, I reached a critical milestone in my journey through the foster care system. Turning eighteen meant I'd face a pivotal decision regarding my future. At this age, individuals have the choice to sign themselves out of the system and step into the world independently or remain within the foster care system, abiding by its existing rules. Recognizing the support and structure it could provide during this crucial transition period, I chose to sign myself back into the system.

I continued living in the transitional home while embarking on the search for my next steps. Life after foster care seemed daunting, and I felt unprepared for what lay ahead. Uncertainty clouded my mind as I pondered about my future. Taking the SATs without much preparation, I surprised myself by achieving a respectable score of 1590; nothing to brag about but still the highest in my graduating class. This accomplishment reaffirmed my intelligence, yet I recognized that I lacked the dedication and motivation to excel academically.

During my time in the transition living home, we actively engaged in activities aimed at fostering independence. Cooking classes were organized to enhance our culinary skills, and the house parents ensured that we had transportation to various destinations, enabling us to explore the world beyond our immediate surroundings. Employment opportunities were also encouraged, and I initially worked at Zaxby's for three months before transitioning to a six-month stint at Burger King. These experiences provided valuable lessons in responsibility, work ethic, and financial independence.

In January or February 2007, an exciting milestone awaited me on my journey—college visits. I had the privilege of exploring three campuses: Columbus State, Morehouse College, and Fort Valley State University. During my visit to Morehouse College, I quickly realized that it didn't resonate with me. The atmosphere, which placed significant emphasis on wealth and material possessions, along with the subpar dormitories, failed to capture my interest. On the other hand, Fort Valley State University was in the process of constructing brand new dormitories for incoming freshmen, and the environment felt more aligned with my personal preferences and values.

The Road to College

A conversation with my caseworker shed light on a potential support system during my college years. She informed me that her family lived near Fort Valley and expressed their willingness to look after me as I pursued my education. This connection solidified my decision to attend Fort Valley State University; located approximately an hour away from Columbus.

May arrived, marking my high school graduation and the commencement of earnest preparations for college. The foster care programs provided invaluable assistance during this time, ensuring I had the necessary resources to embark on this new chapter. I received essential school supplies, guidance in opening a bank account, a laptop for academic pursuits, and furniture to furnish my dorm room. Armed with these essential tools, I moved seamlessly from the transitional living home to college life.

Transitioning to College

I moved into the college dormitories in August of 2007, eager to embark on this new chapter of my life. However, the initial semester proved to be a challenging adjustment. Suddenly faced with the responsibility of managing my own schedule and making independent decisions, I found myself in unfamiliar territory. Until that point, I had not shouldered significant responsibilities. Navigating this newfound freedom, I became somewhat antisocial, often retreating to the confines of my dorm room. My focus shifted away from academic pursuits, and I spent a considerable amount of time engrossed in video games, losing sight of my educational goals.

The consequences of my lack of focus and dedication during my initial semester of college became undeniable when I received academic probation with a disheartening GPA of 1.7. It was a wake-up call that shook me to my core. The realization hit me that I was jeopardizing my future and wasting the opportunities that had been given to me.

However, it was also during this challenging period that I had the privilege of meeting my caseworker's family, who would become instrumental in my journey. They had been a source of support throughout my transition to college, and their impact became even more profound during this difficult time. Recognizing the genuine concern they had for my academic progress, they took the initiative to review my grades at the end of the semester. Their unwavering belief in my potential and their genuine care for my well-being shone through their actions. They understood the importance of intervention and provided me with the additional support and guidance I desperately needed.

The Road to College

Their mentorship and investment in my success sparked a newfound determination within me. Their willingness to dedicate their time and energy to help me get back on track academically instilled a sense of responsibility and accountability. I realized that I couldn't afford to squander this opportunity for a brighter future.

With their guidance, I developed a strategic plan to improve my academic performance. We established a study schedule and created a supportive environment conducive to learning. They helped me identify resources on campus, such as tutoring services and study groups, and encouraged me to seek help when needed. They also emphasized the importance of time management and prioritization, helping me strike a balance between my studies and other aspects of college life.

Their involvement didn't stop at academics. They also provided emotional support, acting as a pillar of strength during moments of doubt and frustration. They reminded me of my resilience and encouraged me to persevere, assuring me that setbacks were a natural part of the journey.

As I implemented the changes and began to take ownership of my education, I witnessed a gradual improvement in my performance. With each passing semester, my grades steadily climbed, and I regained my sense of purpose and dedication. The support and mentorship I received from my caseworker's family were invaluable in helping me regain my footing and thrive in the college environment.

Beyond the academic realm, my involvement in campus activities and student organizations further enriched my college experience. I sought out opportunities to make meaningful connections with fellow students, faculty, and staff. Through these interactions, I broadened my horizons, gained valuable insights, and developed lifelong friendships.

The first year of college became a transformative period in my life. It taught me the importance of resilience, perseverance, and seeking support when needed. It was a year of self-discovery and personal growth, as I learned to navigate challenges, overcome obstacles, and make the most of the opportunities presented to me.

Lack of Guidance

One of the significant obstacles I encountered during my college journey was the lack of guidance and career exploration. No one had taken the time to sit me down and have a meaningful conversation about the various career options available to me. As a result, I found myself blindly selecting a major without a

The Road to College

clear understanding of where it would lead me.

When I initially entered college, I chose to pursue a business marketing major. It seemed like a practical choice at the time, with the potential for future employment opportunities. However, as I progressed through my coursework, I quickly realized that it didn't align with my interests and passions. The classes felt uninspiring, and I struggled to find meaning in the material.

During my junior year, I enrolled in an intro accounting course, hoping it would provide me with a better understanding of the business world. However, it became evident that accounting was not the right fit for me either. The numbers and formulas felt monotonous, and I yearned for something more intellectually stimulating. It was at this point that I began to question my career path and started exploring other options.

It was during this period of self-reflection that I discovered my genuine love for history. I found myself captivated by the stories of the past, the lessons they held, and the opportunity to delve into the complexities of human civilization. The decision to switch my major to history was driven by a deep passion for the subject matter. I felt a sense of excitement and fulfillment that I hadn't experienced before in my academic pursuits.

However, despite my newfound enthusiasm for history,

Against All Odds

I faced uncertainty about the practical applications of a history degree. I questioned what career opportunities would be available to me and how I could translate my academic knowledge into a fulfilling and sustainable profession. This uncertainty led me to briefly switch my major to education in 2012, hoping that it would offer a more direct path to a career.

Nevertheless, after further consideration and exploration, I ultimately decided to switch back to history. I couldn't deny my passion for the subject, and I believed that by pursuing what I loved, I would find a way to carve out a meaningful career path. I realized that the value of a degree is not solely determined by its direct career prospects but also by the skills, knowledge, and critical thinking abilities it instills.

The constant changes in my major, coupled with the lack of career guidance, resulted in an extended undergraduate journey that spanned six and a half years. It was a journey filled with trial and error, as I searched for the right academic path that aligned with both my interests and my future aspirations. At times, I felt frustrated and uncertain about the future, questioning whether I was making the right choices.

Looking back, I realize that the absence of career guidance had a significant impact on the duration of my undergraduate studies. Had I received proper guidance and mentorship earlier on, I might have been able to make more informed decisions about my major and chart a more direct path towards graduation. I understand the importance of seeking advice from mentors, career counselors, and professionals in the field to gain insights into various career paths and make informed decisions about my academic pursuits.

However, despite the challenges and the prolonged timeline, my journey through college taught me valuable lessons about self-discovery, resilience, and the importance of finding true passion and purpose in one's chosen field of study. It was a time of exploration and growth, where I learned to embrace change, adapt to new circumstances, and persevere in the face of obstacles.

In the end, my meandering path through different majors ultimately led me to my true calling in history, and I emerged from my undergraduate studies with a deep love for the subject and a clearer sense of the possibilities it held for my future. The lessons I learned during those six and a half years continue to shape my perspective and drive my pursuit of knowledge and personal fulfillment. I understand the value of following my passions and striving for a career that aligns with my interests and values, even if it means taking a less conventional or more challenging path.

Against All Odds

The Beginning of my Future

In 2010, I made the decision to join the ROTC (Reserve Officers' Training Corps), which marked a significant turning point in my college experience. At the time, I was 5'9" and weighed 245 pounds, realizing that I was not only overweight but also leading an unhealthy lifestyle. Joining the ROTC presented an opportunity for me to pursue my interest in the military while simultaneously addressing my need for structure and discipline in my life.

Enlisting in the military was not my desired path, but through the ROTC, I could gain a comprehensive understanding of military structure and principles. It provided me with a structured environment that I lacked, instilling a sense of responsibility and accountability. The ROTC became a foundational pillar in my college journey, shaping my character and guiding my personal growth.

Initially, I committed myself to a two-year program with the intention of commissioning in 2012. However, I encountered challenges along the way due to my failure to attend mandatory events, which led to a suspension for one year. This setback served as a valuable lesson in the importance of commitment and punctuality. It made me realize the significance of honoring obligations and prioritizing responsibilities.

The Road to College

After serving my suspension, I returned to the ROTC program in August 2012. During the summer of 2013, I attended cadet camp, which provided me with invaluable training and further solidified my understanding of military principles and practices. In May 2014, I successfully graduated from college and received my commission, marking the culmination of my ROTC journey.

Throughout my college years, my living arrangements varied. For the first two years, I resided on campus, immersing myself in the college environment and fostering connections with fellow students. During one of those years, I took summer classes to continue progressing academically. Additionally, I worked as a resident assistant during one summer, allowing me to stay in the dorms for free during the break, which helped alleviate financial burdens.

However, after 2010, I made the decision to move off-campus. This decision meant that during holidays and breaks, I had to rely on the hospitality of mentors or find temporary accommodations elsewhere. Despite the challenges of finding suitable housing during breaks, I remained dedicated to my education and persevered through the various obstacles that came my way.

To support myself financially throughout college, I

worked a variety of jobs. I held positions at Burger King, participated in work-study programs on campus, and even worked at JC Penney. These jobs provided me with valuable life skills, taught me the importance of time management, and helped me finance my education. While I wasn't on a scholarship, I took out loans and paid my way through college, demonstrating my commitment to obtaining a degree.

The combination of my involvement in the ROTC, various living arrangements, and my work experiences shaped my college experience into a unique journey of personal growth, discipline, and financial responsibility. It taught me the value of perseverance, adaptability, and the importance of seizing opportunities for self-improvement. Despite the challenges I faced, I emerged from college with a stronger sense of purpose, a well-rounded skill set, and the determination to overcome any obstacles that may come my way.

Navigating the Transition from Foster Care to Adulthood

Honestly, foster care did not adequately prepare me to be a successful, functioning citizen. I didn't know how to manage my time, and I didn't know how to manage my health. I was so accustomed to being told what to do constantly, not having access to things I needed, and living in a survivalist mindset, that it took me several of those college years to learn how to function as an adult.

The transition from foster care to adulthood presented a unique set of challenges that I was ill-prepared to face. The lack of stability and guidance during my formative years left me with gaps in essential life skills that many young adults take for granted. Time management, in particular, was a struggle for me. In foster care, my days were often structured for me, and I didn't have to worry about planning my schedule or prioritizing tasks. As a result, I found it difficult to balance my academic responsibilities, work commitments, and personal life.

Additionally, managing my health became a challenge. In foster care, access to healthcare and healthy habits were not consistently prioritized. I lacked the knowledge and skills to take care of my physical and mental well-being effectively. It took time for me to learn how to establish healthy routines, seek medical care when needed, and prioritize self-care amidst the demands of college life.

Moreover, the survivalist mindset that developed during my time in foster care influenced my approach to adulthood. I was accustomed to scarcity, and the fear of not having enough resources or support lingered in the back of my mind. This mindset affected my decision-making and hindered my ability to fully embrace opportunities and take risks. It took me a while to shift my perspective, build confidence, and believe that I had the capacity to thrive in the world beyond foster care.

Over the course of my college years, I gradually learned to navigate these challenges and develop the skills necessary to function as an independent adult. I sought guidance from mentors, utilized campus resources, and actively sought out opportunities for personal growth. Through trial and error, I discovered strategies that worked for me, such as creating structured schedules, practicing self-care, and seeking support when needed.

Reflecting on my journey, I recognize the need for improved support systems and resources for young adults transitioning out of foster care. It is crucial to provide comprehensive life skills training, mentorship, and ongoing support to help these individuals bridge the gap and navigate the complexities of adulthood successfully. Addressing the unique challenges faced by former foster youth can empower them to overcome obstacles, reach their full potential, and thrive in their chosen paths.

Despite the difficulties I encountered, my college experience became a transformative period of growth and learning. It taught me resilience, adaptability, and the importance of seeking help when needed. I emerged from those years with a newfound sense of independence, self-confidence, and a determination to create a fulfilling and meaningful life for myself. My journey serves as a reminder that with the right support and a willingness to learn and grow, individuals from foster care backgrounds can overcome their unique challenges and achieve their goals.

Chapter 6: Life After College

Graduation and Commission

The day I graduated from college marked another significant turning point in my life. It was a momentous occasion that coincided with my commissioning into the military. Looking back, the path that unfolded before me was unexpected but filled with gratitude, as it set the stage for a transformative journey. May of 2014 became a powerful symbol of transition and new beginnings, shaping the trajectory of my future.

In 2014, I began my military journey by joining the National Guard, embarking on a path that would test and shape me in ways I had never imagined. This phase commenced with a rigorous 16-week basic course held at Fort Leavenworth, Missouri, spanning from March to July 2015. The training was intense, pushing me both physically and mentally, but it instilled in me the discipline, resilience, and teamwork necessary for military service.

During this period, I also pursued a regular job as an assistant manager at Sherwin Williams. Balancing my civilian employment with military obligations allowed me to develop a diverse skill set and gain valuable experiences in both realms. At Sherwin Williams, I engaged in sales-related responsibilities, honing my interpersonal and leadership skills while managing a team and serving customers. This dual experience provided a unique perspective and a foundation of adaptability that would prove invaluable throughout my military career.

In May of 2017, I decided to transition to active duty. At that time, there was a request for National Guard members to join the active-duty ranks, and I was intrigued by the prospect of further challenge and opportunities. Fueled by a desire for personal growth and a deeper commitment to service, I submitted a comprehensive packet that included letters of recommendation and other necessary documentation.

In response to my submission, I received a list of potential deployment locations. Carefully considering the options before me, I weighed the opportunities and responsibilities each destination presented. After thoughtful deliberation, I chose to be stationed in South Korea. The chance to immerse myself in a different culture while fulfilling my military duties was an enticing prospect that promised to broaden my horizons and deepen my understanding of the world.

With the decision made, I embarked on my active-duty assignment, commencing in 2017 and extending into 2018. However, before delving into the specifics of my time in South Korea, it is important to acknowledge the early years of my military journey. The National Guard experience taught me the importance of discipline, teamwork, and adaptability. It provided a solid foundation upon which I would build my career, shaping my character and instilling in me a profound sense of duty.

During my early years in the military, I developed a deep appreciation for the camaraderie and bond among service members. The shared experiences, challenges, and triumphs forged lasting connections and a sense of belonging within a community dedicated to a common purpose. I learned the value of relying on others and being relied upon, fostering a spirit of teamwork that would prove essential in the years to come.

Those formative years also refined my leadership skills. Whether it was leading a team during training exercises or taking on responsibilities in my civilian job, I learned the importance of effective communication, decision-making, and inspiring others to perform at their best. These skills would continue to evolve and shape my ability to lead throughout my military career.

In essence, the day of my college graduation marked the beginning of a remarkable journey in the military. The early years spent in the National Guard set the groundwork for the challenges and opportunities that lay ahead. It was during this time that I learned the fundamental principles of military service, gained invaluable experiences, and honed the skills necessary to thrive in a demanding and ever-changing environment. These early experiences served as a solid foundation as I transitioned into active duty and embarked on the next chapter of my military career.

South Korea

From 2017 to 2018, I had the privilege of residing in South Korea and serving in an aviation unit with a critical mission: to provide vital aviation assets in the event of a potential conflict with North Korea. This period was incredibly meaningful to me, as it allowed me to immerse myself in an environment that constantly challenged me and provided opportunities for personal and professional growth.

Within the aviation unit, I held the crucial position of a

weapons of mass destruction defense analyst. This role required me to have a comprehensive understanding of North Korea's weapons capabilities, their potential impact on our aviation assets, and the ability to provide invaluable analysis to my senior-level commanders. I took this responsibility to heart, knowing that the information and insights I contributed were instrumental in shaping our preparedness and ensuring the safety of our forces.

To maintain the highest level of readiness, we engaged in numerous emergency deployment readiness exercises (EDRES). These exercises, held in the early hours of the morning, simulated the intensity and urgency of potential combat scenarios. Participating in these exercises was physically and mentally demanding, requiring unwavering focus, attention to detail, and the ability to perform under pressure. However, the challenges and sacrifices were always outweighed by the sense of purpose and fulfillment that came with knowing we were constantly honing our skills and maintaining a state of readiness for any eventuality.

Despite the demanding nature of my duties, I found great fulfillment in my role as a weapons of mass destruction defense analyst. The camaraderie and strong bonds I formed with my colleagues and superiors were invaluable. We shared a common purpose and a deep sense of commitment to our mission, fostering an environment of trust, support, and collaboration. Together, we faced challenges head-on, relying on each other's expertise and collective strength to overcome obstacles and achieve our objectives.

In the moments of respite from our demanding tasks, I seized every opportunity to explore and embrace the rich culture of South Korea. I reveled in the vibrant traditions, historical landmarks, and warmth of the local community. The diverse cuisine tantalized my taste buds, and I savored every culinary experience, discovering new flavors and expanding my palate. These moments of cultural immersion served as a reminder of the privilege and unique opportunity I had been afforded to not only serve my country but also to broaden my horizons and deepen my understanding of the world.

As a CBRN (Chemical, Biological, Radiological, and Nuclear) officer, I cherished the respite from the constant barrage of negative news from back home. It provided me with the space to focus wholeheartedly on my mission, free from distractions and the weight of external events. In that environment, I found a renewed sense of purpose and dedication to my work. It was a time when I could fully appreciate the significance of what I was doing and the impact it could have on the safety and well-being of our forces.

Life After College

The period I spent in South Korea during my military service holds a special place in my heart. It was a time of personal growth, professional development, and unforgettable experiences. The challenges I faced, the bonds I formed, and the cultural immersion I embraced all contributed to a profound appreciation and love for that chapter of my military journey. It laid the foundation for my future years of service, shaping my character, enhancing my skills, and instilling in me a lifelong commitment to serve and pursue excellence.

Fort Hood, Texas

After my rewarding experience serving in South Korea, I returned to the United States and was stationed at Fort Hood, Texas from 2018 to 2021. This transition brought fresh challenges and opportunities to my military career, as I found myself amidst a dynamic and bustling military community.

Fort Hood housed a diverse range of units, making it a vibrant environment for professional growth and collaboration. The base's size and scope provided ample opportunities to interact with fellow service members from different branches and specialties. This diversity of expertise and perspectives enriched our collective knowledge and fostered an atmosphere of cooperation and mutual support.

During my time at Fort Hood, I had the privilege of serving in a role that allowed me to continue contributing to the overall mission readiness of our forces. Whether it was through training exercises, operational planning, or conducting evaluations, I remained dedicated to ensuring our unit maintained the highest level of preparedness. The sense of purpose and responsibility that came with this role motivated me to constantly seek out new training opportunities and resources.

Fort Hood proved to be a hub of professional development, offering an array of training programs designed to enhance our skills and knowledge. I actively participated in various specialized training courses, which focused on areas such as tactical operations, leadership development, and advanced weaponry systems. These experiences not only expanded my capabilities but also provided me with a solid foundation for my future assignments. The base's commitment to continuous learning and improvement allowed us to stay at the forefront of military tactics and technology.

Beyond the professional realm, Fort Hood provided a vibrant and close-knit community that played a significant role in the lives of service members and their families. The camaraderie among fellow soldiers and their loved ones fostered a strong sense of belonging and mutual support. Engaging in social activities, participating in community events, and forging connections with others enriched my overall experience at Fort Hood. Whether it was attending unit functions, recreational sports leagues, or volunteering in the local community, these activities allowed us to bond and create lasting friendships.

The base also recognized the importance of supporting military families. Fort Hood provided a range of services and programs tailored to the needs of families, including childcare facilities, educational resources, and spouse support groups. This commitment to family well-being created a supportive environment that allowed service members to focus on their duties, while knowing that their loved ones were well taken care of.

Located in close proximity to the city of Killeen and its surrounding communities, Fort Hood presented opportunities to explore the unique Texan culture and experience the hospitality of the locals. Venturing off the base allowed me to sample the delicious Tex-Mex cuisine, attend local festivals, and engage in outdoor activities such as hiking and fishing. These experiences not only provided a well-deserved break from our rigorous schedules but also allowed us to connect with the local community and appreciate the rich heritage of the region.

Fort Riley, Kansas

In 2021, my military journey transported me to Fort Riley, located in Manhattan, Kansas. This new station offered a different setting and presented a unique set of opportunities for me to continue my professional growth. Fort Riley is widely recognized for its rich history and its role as the home of the 1st Infantry Division, famously known as the "Big Red One."

Being stationed at Fort Riley provided me with the chance to further develop my leadership skills as I assumed roles of increasing responsibility. Working alongside dedicated and talented soldiers, I engaged in missions and training exercises that focused on maintaining combat readiness and upholding the highest standards of performance. Collaborating with my fellow service members allowed us to sharpen our skills, refine our teamwork, and ensure that we were prepared for any potential challenges.

Living in Manhattan, Kansas, I had the privilege of experiencing the warmth and hospitality of the local community. The residents of Manhattan showed unwavering support and appreciation towards the military, which created a strong bond between the military personnel and the local community. This connection fostered a sense of unity and mutual respect, making Fort Riley feel like a home away from home. Whether it was attending community events, engaging in volunteer activities, or simply interacting with the locals, the strong support from the community made a positive impact on our morale and well-being.

Throughout my time at Fort Riley, I continued to grow both personally and professionally. The challenges and experiences I encountered further shaped my character, resilience, and adaptability. I embraced the opportunity to learn from seasoned professionals, mentor junior soldiers, and contribute to the overall success of the mission. The rich history and traditions of Fort Riley, combined with the dedication and professionalism of the soldiers stationed there, provided an environment that fostered growth and excellence.

I seized every chance to expand my knowledge and skills through specialized training programs and professional development opportunities. These initiatives allowed me to stay current with the latest tactics, techniques, and technologies in my field. Additionally, I actively sought out leadership positions that enabled me to refine my decision-making abilities, strengthen my communication skills, and inspire others to achieve their full potential.

The time spent at Fort Riley not only offered professional growth but also provided opportunities for personal fulfillment. Exploring the scenic beauty of Kansas, engaging in outdoor activities, and participating in cultural events enriched my overall experience. The close-knit military community at Fort Riley, combined with the support of the local community, created an environment that encouraged collaboration, camaraderie, and personal connections.

Current Life

However, due to persistent injuries, I have been honorably discharged from the military, marking both the end of a chapter and the beginning of a new phase in my life. While it is a bittersweet conclusion to my military career, I am immensely grateful for the experiences, opportunities, and the unwavering support I received during my service.

In addition to receiving an honorable discharge, I completed a master's degree in emergency management and have started a second master's degree in Intelligence Analysis at Johns Hopkins

Life After College

University. This academic pursuit has provided me with a renewed sense of purpose and direction during this professional transition. Delving deeper into a specialized subject of great personal interest has allowed me to expand my knowledge and gain a deeper understanding of the world around me. I am grateful for the support and understanding of my professors, mentors, and peers throughout this academic journey, as they have played a crucial role in my continued growth and development.

I am currently preparing to move into my new home in Nebraska to work for the Air Force as an Emergency Management Specialist. Although my military career has come to an end, I view this transition as an opportunity for growth and reinvention. The combination of my military experience, academic achievements, and unwavering determination will serve as a strong foundation for future endeavors. I am eager to apply the knowledge and skills gained through my master's degree in practical settings, contributing meaningfully to society in a different capacity.

While the conclusion of my military career and the limitations met by my injuries have brought about unexpected changes, I remain steadfast in my commitment to service and the values instilled in me during my time in the military. The resilience, discipline, and dedication acquired throughout my military journey will continue to guide me as I navigate this new chapter. I am determined to make a positive impact in both my professional and personal life, utilizing the experiences, values, and education that have shaped my journey thus far.

As I embark on this new chapter, I am grateful for the support and understanding of my fellow service members, friends, and family who have stood by me during this challenging period. Their unwavering encouragement and belief in my abilities have been invaluable, providing solace and strength as I navigate this transition. The foster kid from Georgia who defied odds and pursued a military career now finds himself on a path filled with unexpected twists and turns. Reflecting on this journey, I am humbled by the opportunities I have been given and excited for the future that lies ahead.

As I embrace new challenges, I am committed to making a difference in the lives of others, inspired by the belief that every setback is an opportunity for growth and that every experience has the potential to shape one's character. The diverse experiences and unique perspective I bring will enable me to contribute to society in meaningful ways, serving as a testament to the resilience and determination that have guided me throughout my life. I am excited to embrace this new chapter and continue making a positive impact on the world around me.

Chapter 7: Advocating for Change

Fostering Stability and Nurturing Environments for Every Child

My reflections based on my experience in foster care are profound and have shaped my perspective on the importance of supportive and stable family environments. Having lived in a staggering number of 25 different homes and attended 13 different schools throughout my life—six elementary schools, five middle schools, and two high schools—the challenges and disruptions I faced have left a lasting impact.

The constant moves and transitions inherent in the foster care system created a sense of instability and dependency. Each new home and school brought with it the need to adapt and adjust to new relationships and unfamiliar surroundings. This constant upheaval made it difficult to establish a sense of belonging and continuity in my life.

It is evident that there is a pressing need for better

families within the foster care system. Children in foster care deserve loving, supportive, and stable homes where they can grow, thrive, and develop a sense of security. The impact of a nurturing family environment cannot be overstated, as it provides the foundation for emotional well-being, educational success, and overall life outcomes.

Advocating for change within the foster care system has become a personal mission of mine. I believe that every child deserves the opportunity to be part of a loving and permanent family, and I am committed to raising awareness about the challenges faced by foster children. By sharing my own story and advocating for reforms, I hope to inspire discussions, policy changes, and community support that will improve the lives of those in foster care.

We need to prioritize the recruitment, training, and support of foster families who are equipped to provide stable and nurturing environments. Additionally, strengthening collaboration between child welfare agencies, schools, and communities can help create a cohesive support system for foster children, ensuring their needs are met holistically.

Advocating for change goes beyond just addressing the immediate needs of foster children; it involves tackling systemic issues and promoting long-term solutions. This includes supporting initiatives that focus on family preservation, early intervention, and comprehensive services to address the underlying factors that contribute to the placement of children in foster care.

Through awareness campaigns, community engagement, and collaborative efforts, we can work towards a foster care system that truly prioritizes the best interests of the children it serves. By advocating for change, we can create a future where every child in foster care has the opportunity to thrive, grow, and reach their full potential within the embrace of a loving and supportive family.

Recognizing the Need for Change

The foster care system, though designed with good intentions, is deeply flawed, and it is crucial that we address the issues that perpetuate dependency and hinder the well-being of foster youth. To create a system that truly nurtures and supports children in need, we must confront these challenges head-on and advocate for meaningful change.

One of the critical issues that need to be addressed is the dependency foster care often creates. Many foster youth experience a constant sense of instability and uncertainty, being moved from one placement to another, sometimes multiple times. This lack of continuity can disrupt their sense of identity, belonging, and overall well-being. To address this, we must prioritize stability and permanency in foster care.

First and foremost, the focus should shift towards finding and supporting true, caring families for foster youth. We need to invest in recruitment efforts that prioritize quality over quantity, ensuring that prospective foster families undergo thorough screenings, training, and receive ongoing support. By prioritizing the well-being and development of foster youth, we can create a nurturing environment that promotes healthy attachments, stability, and a sense of belonging.

Moreover, we must prioritize kinship placements whenever possible. Placing children with relatives or extended family members can help maintain important familial and cultural connections, providing a stronger foundation for their emotional well-being. By providing adequate support services and resources to kinship caregivers, we can strengthen these placements and enhance the chances of long-term success.

In addition to promoting stable family placements, we need to address the lack of resources and support available to foster families. Foster parents often face overwhelming challenges in meeting the complex needs of the children in their care. Increasing access to high-quality training, mental health services, and respite care for foster families can alleviate some of these burdens and promote healthier, more effective caregiving.

Furthermore, we must prioritize the emotional well-being of foster youth by providing them with comprehensive mental health services and therapeutic support. Many children in foster care have experienced trauma, abuse, and neglect, and it is crucial that they receive appropriate interventions to address their unique needs. By investing in trauma-informed care and mental health services, we can help foster youth heal and develop resilience.

To empower foster youth towards independence, we need to prioritize education and life skills training. Ensuring educational stability and continuity, providing academic support, and equipping youth with essential life skills will enhance their self-confidence and increase their chances of success as they transition into adulthood. Programs that promote higher education, vocational training, and mentorship opportunities can also play a vital role in preparing foster youth for independent living.

Additionally, we must address the systemic issues that contribute to the overrepresentation of marginalized communities within the foster care system. Poverty, racial disparities, and social inequalities often intersect, leading to a disproportionate number of children from these communities entering foster care. Once we address these root causes and advocate for equitable social policies, we can work towards preventing unnecessary family separations and reducing the need for foster care.

Addressing Systemic Issues and Long-Term Solutions

While it is crucial to focus on immediate needs and provide support for children in foster care, it is equally important to address the systemic issues that contribute to the challenges they face. By tackling these underlying problems, we can work towards long-term solutions that prevent unnecessary family separations and create a more equitable foster care system.

The overrepresentation of marginalized communities within the foster care system needs to be addressed. Poverty, racial disparities, and social inequalities often intersect, leading to a disproportionate number

Advocating for Change

of children from these communities entering foster care. To address this, we must advocate for equitable social policies that promote economic opportunities, access to quality education, affordable housing, and healthcare. By addressing the root causes of family instability and providing support to at-risk families, we can help prevent the need for children to enter foster care in the first place.

Another important aspect is family preservation. Many families struggle with issues such as substance abuse, mental health challenges, or domestic violence, which can put children at risk of removal. By investing in early intervention programs and providing comprehensive support services to families, we can help them address these underlying issues and create a safe and nurturing environment for their children. This may include access to substance abuse treatment, mental health counseling, parenting support, and domestic violence prevention programs. Offering these services proactively can help prevent unnecessary family separations and promote family reunification when it is safe and appropriate.

Furthermore, foster care agencies should prioritize kinship placements whenever possible. Placing children with relatives or extended family members not only helps maintain important familial and cultural connections, but it also provides a more stable and supportive environment for the child. To facilitate kinship placements, it is crucial to provide adequate support services to kinship caregivers, including financial assistance, respite care, and access to training and resources. By strengthening the kinship care system, we can improve outcomes for children in foster care and reduce the strain on traditional foster families.

Additionally, it is important to improve collaboration and coordination among child welfare agencies, schools, and communities. Many children in foster care face significant educational challenges due to frequent moves and disruptions in their schooling. Enhancing communication and information sharing between entities ensures educational stability and continuity for foster youth. This may include developing individualized education plans, providing academic support services, and addressing any special needs or learning disabilities.

Lastly, we must prioritize the transition of foster youth into adulthood. Many young people who age out of the foster care system face significant challenges as they navigate the transition to independent living. To support their successful transition, we should focus on providing comprehensive life skills training, access to higher education or vocational training, and mentorship opportunities.

 **By equipping foster youth with the necessary tools and resources, we can empower them to become self-sufficient and lead fulfilling lives.**

Addressing systemic issues within the foster care system requires a comprehensive and collaborative approach. It involves advocating for policy changes, allocating resources to support at-risk families, and promoting community engagement and awareness.

Addressing these underlying issues will create a foster care system that not only responds to immediate needs but also strives for long-term solutions, ensuring the well-being and success of every child in foster care.

Empowering Foster Youth towards Independence

Empowering foster youth towards independence requires prioritizing education and life skills training. Education serves as a powerful tool for breaking the cycle of dependency and opening doors to a brighter future. However, foster youth often face significant educational challenges due to frequent moves, disruptions in schooling, and the trauma they have experienced. Therefore, it is crucial to prioritize educational stability and continuity for these young individuals.

Ensuring that foster youth have access to quality education begins with addressing the factors that disrupt their schooling. Collaborative efforts between child welfare agencies and schools can play a crucial role in mitigating these challenges. By sharing information and working together, it is possible to identify and implement strategies that minimize disruptions, such as coordinating school transfers, ensuring timely enrollment, and maintaining communication between school personnel and foster parents.

Moreover, providing academic support tailored to the unique needs of foster youth is vital. Many of these young individuals require additional assistance to catch up and thrive academically. Implementing programs that offer tutoring, mentoring, and academic counseling can make a significant difference in their educational journeys. Additionally, providing access to specialized services, such as special education resources or trauma-informed instruction, can help address the specific needs of foster youth and support their educational success.

Advocating for Change

Beyond academic support, equipping foster youth with essential life skills is crucial for their successful transition into adulthood. Life skills training should encompass a wide range of practical knowledge, including financial literacy, job readiness, problem-solving, communication, and self-care skills. These skills empower foster youth to navigate the challenges of independent living, make informed decisions, and better advocate for themselves. Life skills training programs can be integrated into the foster care system, providing workshops, classes, or mentorship opportunities that offer guidance and support on various aspects of adult life.

Higher education and vocational training programs are also instrumental in preparing foster youth for independent living. Access to post-secondary education should be actively promoted, along with financial assistance, scholarships, and grants that are readily available to support their pursuit of higher education. Additionally, vocational training and apprenticeship programs can provide valuable alternatives for those who prefer a more hands-on approach to acquiring skills and entering the workforce. Collaboration with educational institutions, community organizations, and employers can expand opportunities and create pathways to success for foster youth.

Finally, mentorship opportunities play a vital role in the

development and success of foster youth. Mentors can provide guidance, support, and a positive role model for young individuals navigating the challenges of foster care and the transition to independence. Mentoring programs, both formal and informal, help connect foster youth with caring adults who can offer guidance, share experiences, and provide a supportive presence in their lives. These relationships can help foster youth build resilience, self-confidence, and a sense of belonging.

Prioritizing education and life skills training, employs foster youth with the tools they need to succeed as they transition into adulthood. Ensuring educational stability, providing academic support, and equipping them with essential life skills are essential components of a comprehensive approach to foster care. Investing in their education, promoting higher education and vocational training, and offering mentorship opportunities will create a foster care system that prepares foster youth for independent living, increases their chances of success, and helps them build a foundation for a fulfilling future.

Advocating for Change

Creating A Future of Opportunity and Support

Creating a future of opportunity and support for foster youth requires a multifaceted approach that addresses their unique needs and challenges. By focusing on key areas such as education, employment, housing, and emotional well-being, we can pave the way for a brighter future and empower foster youth to thrive as they transition into adulthood.

Education plays a pivotal role in unlocking opportunities for foster youth. It is crucial to ensure that they have access to quality education and the necessary support to succeed academically. This involves promoting educational stability by minimizing disruptions caused by placement changes and providing educational resources tailored to their needs. Collaborative efforts between child welfare agencies, schools, and educators can help create systems that prioritize the educational well-being of foster youth, including individualized education plans, academic support services, and targeted interventions for those who may have fallen behind. Investing in their education, sets foster youth up with the knowledge and skills they will need to pursue their aspirations and build a strong foundation for their future.

Employment opportunities are another essential aspect of creating a future of opportunity for foster youth.

Against All Odds

Transitioning into the workforce can be challenging for young individuals who have experienced instability and may lack a strong support system. To address this, it is crucial to provide vocational training, job readiness programs, and career counseling tailored to the specific needs of foster youth. Collaborations with local businesses, organizations, and government agencies can create internship programs, apprenticeships, and job placement opportunities, enabling foster youth to gain valuable work experience and develop the skills necessary for long-term success. Promoting employment opportunities helps empower foster youth to achieve economic independence and build a solid foundation for their future well-being.

Access to safe and stable housing is another critical factor in supporting foster youth's successful transition to adulthood. Many foster youth face housing instabilities as they age out of the system, increasing their vulnerability and hindering their ability to thrive. To address this, it is essential to establish comprehensive housing programs and initiatives targeted specifically at supporting foster youth. This may include transitional housing options, rental assistance, and access to affordable housing. Collaborations between housing agencies, community organizations, and foster care systems can help ensure that foster youth have access to safe, stable, and affordable housing options as they navigate the transition into independent living.

Advocating for Change

Emotional well-being is a fundamental aspect of creating a future of support for foster youth. Many foster youth experience trauma, loss, and instability, which can have long-lasting effects on their mental health. It is crucial to prioritize trauma-informed care and provide comprehensive mental health services that address their unique needs. This may involve access to therapy, counseling, and support groups that help foster youth process their experiences, develop coping mechanisms, and build resilience. Additionally, mentorship programs and peer support networks can provide vital emotional support and guidance as foster youth navigate the challenges of adulthood. By prioritizing their emotional well-being, we empower foster youth to overcome adversity and build a strong foundation for their future success.

Creating a future of opportunity and support for foster youth requires collaboration and coordination among child welfare agencies, educational institutions, employers, housing providers, and mental health professionals. We must invest in their education, promote employment opportunities, and ensure access to safe and stable housing, and prioritizing their emotional well-being, we can empower foster youth to reach their full potential and create a brighter future for themselves. Together, we can build a foster care system that provides the necessary tools, resources, and support to help foster youth thrive as they transition into adulthood.

Chapter 8: To My Fellow Foster Youth

This section is dedicated to you—my fellow foster youth who are walking a path that, at times, feels treacherous and unforgiving. I want you to know that you are not alone in your struggles, and that within you lies a remarkable strength that can weather any storm. As you navigate the complexities of the foster care system, I offer you these words of encouragement, resilience, and hope.

Your Worth and Potential

First and foremost, I want you to understand that your worth and potential are immeasurable. It is essential to recognize that the circumstances that led you into foster care do not define who you are as a person. The brokenness of the system or the hardships you have endured are not a reflection of your value or your potential for success.

Against All Odds

You are not defined by the challenges you have faced or the difficulties you have overcome. Instead, you are defined by the fire that burns within you—the fire of resilience, determination, and strength. It is this fire that refuses to be extinguished, no matter the obstacles that come your way.

Every foster youth possesses unique qualities, talents, and abilities that make them special. Your past experiences, though they may have been tough, have shaped you into a remarkable individual. The strength you have displayed in navigating through difficult circumstances is a testament to your inherent worth.

It is important to remember that your worth goes beyond the circumstances of your upbringing. You have the power to shape your own future and define your own identity. The challenges you have faced may have temporarily overshadowed your sense of self, but they do not diminish your value as a human being.

Your potential is limitless. You have within you the capacity to achieve great things, to pursue your dreams, and to make a positive impact in the world. The fire that burns within you can be harnessed to fuel your ambitions, to drive your determination, and to propel you towards a future filled with success and

To My Fellow Foster Youth

fulfillment.

As you continue your journey, remind yourself of your immeasurable worth. Embrace the qualities that make you unique and special. Recognize that your past does not dictate your future. You have the power to overcome any obstacles and to create a life that reflects your true potential.

Surround yourself with people who believe in you and support your dreams. Seek out mentors, teachers, or friends who can help you nurture your talents and guide you towards opportunities for growth. Remember that you are not alone on this journey. There are individuals who see your worth and are willing to stand by you as you strive for greatness.

Believe in yourself, even when others may doubt you. Embrace your strengths and celebrate your achievements, no matter how small they may seem. Each step forward is a testament to your resilience and determination.

Never forget that your worth and potential are immeasurable. You have the power to rise above your circumstances and create a future that is filled with joy, success, and fulfillment. The fire within you will continue to burn brightly, lighting the path towards a life that reflects your true worth and potential.

Against All Odds

Embracing Resilience

It is important to acknowledge the inherent difficulties and complexities of the journey you are on as a foster youth. The path you walk is not easy; it is marked by uncertainty, constant changes, and a longing for stability that can be overwhelming at times. However, I want you to remember, my friend, that within you lies a resilience that is unmatched.

You have already overcome so much in your life, and that in itself is a testament to your strength and inner fortitude. The challenges you have faced, the adversities you have navigated, and the obstacles you have surmounted are a reflection of your unwavering spirit. Take solace in the fact that you possess the capacity to endure and rise above the challenges you face.

Resilience is not just about bouncing back from difficult situations; it is about growing and thriving in the face of adversity. It is the ability to adapt, to persevere, and to find strength in the midst of uncertainty. You have proven time and again that you possess this extraordinary resilience.

Remember the moments when you thought you couldn't go on, yet you found the strength within you to keep pushing forward. Recall the times when you felt overwhelmed, but you discovered the resilience to rise above the circumstances and continue on your journey. These experiences are a testament to your ability to overcome and thrive.

Embracing resilience means recognizing that setbacks and challenges are not permanent. They are temporary roadblocks that can be overcome through your indomitable spirit. It means acknowledging that you have the power to rewrite your narrative and shape your own destiny.

In moments of doubt or difficulty, take a moment to reflect on your past successes. Remind yourself of the times when you defied the odds and surpassed expectations. Let these memories serve as a wellspring of motivation and inspiration, reminding you of your inherent strength.

Surround yourself with a support system that uplifts and encourages you. Seek out mentors, friends, or foster care professionals who understand your journey and can provide guidance and assistance along the way. Together, you can navigate the challenges and draw strength from each other's resilience.

When faced with adversity, remember that you have within you the resilience to endure and rise above. Embrace your experiences as opportunities for growth and learning. Every obstacle you overcome only strengthens your resilience and prepares you for the next chapter of your journey.

Believe in yourself, my fellow foster youth. Embrace your resilience as a badge of honor, a testament to your unwavering spirit. You have already proven your ability to overcome and thrive. Trust in your strength, keep moving forward, and know that you have the power to create a future that is filled with hope, joy, and fulfillment.

Nurturing Dreams

In the midst of the chaos and uncertainty that often accompanies the foster care journey, it is crucial to hold on tightly to your dreams. Your dreams are not mere fantasies or illusions; they are the seeds of possibility that have the power to transform your life. Let them be the guiding light that illuminates your path, even in the darkest moments.

Your dreams possess a remarkable ability to transcend your circumstances. They can transport you beyond the limitations of your current situation and offer a glimpse of a brighter future. When everything else seems lost, your dreams can provide you with a sense of hope, purpose, and motivation.

To My Fellow Foster Youth

Embrace your dreams with open arms. Recognize that they are not frivolous or unattainable, but rather the fuel that propels your determination to create a better future for yourself. They are the visions of what is possible; the aspirations that ignite your passion and drive you forward.

Nurturing your dreams requires dedication and commitment. It involves setting goals, breaking them down into manageable steps, and taking action to bring them closer to reality. It means investing time and effort into acquiring the knowledge and skills necessary to pursue your dreams.

In the face of adversity, your dreams provide a sense of direction and purpose. They can serve as a compass, guiding you through the challenges and setbacks that may arise. When the path ahead seems uncertain, let your dreams be the lighthouse that guides you back to your true north.

Surround yourself with individuals who believe in your dreams and support your aspirations. Seek out mentors, teachers, or friends who can provide guidance, encouragement, and valuable insights. Share your dreams with those who understand the power of vision and who can help you nurture them along the way.

Remember, dreams are not static. They evolve and grow as you do. Allow yourself the freedom to adapt and refine your dreams as you gain new experiences and insights. Embrace the journey of discovery and growth that comes with pursuing your dreams. Nurturing your dreams also involves self-care and self-belief. Take care of your physical and emotional well-being, as they form the foundation upon which your dreams can flourish. Cultivate self-confidence and resilience, knowing that you have what it takes to overcome obstacles and turn your dreams into reality.

In the midst of chaos and uncertainty, never let go of your dreams. Let them be the beacon of hope that illuminates your path. Nurture them with unwavering determination and dedication. Embrace the transformative power they hold and allow them to fuel your journey towards a future that surpasses your wildest imagination.

Seeking Support

In your journey as a foster youth, it is crucial to seek out the support that is available to you. Recognize that you do not have to navigate this path alone. Whether it is a caring adult, a mentor, a caseworker, or a support group, surrounding yourself with people who believe in you and your potential can make a significant difference.

Seeking support is not a sign of weakness; it is an act of courage and self-care. It takes strength to acknowledge when you need assistance and to reach out for help. Remember that you are not burdening others by seeking support; in fact, you are giving them the opportunity to make a positive impact in your life.

Identify the individuals or organizations in your life that can provide guidance, encouragement, and practical assistance. Seek out mentors who can offer wisdom and support as you navigate the challenges of foster care. Look for caring adults who can serve as a stable presence in your life, offering guidance and emotional support.

Caseworkers are valuable resources who can connect you with essential services, advocate on your behalf, and provide a listening ear when you need someone to talk to. They are trained professionals who have dedicated their careers to supporting youth in foster care, and they are there to help you.

Consider joining a support group specifically designed for foster youth. These groups provide a safe space for you to share your experiences, hear from others who have gone through similar challenges, and receive encouragement from peers who understand your journey firsthand. The sense of community and understanding can be incredibly empowering.

When reaching out for support, remember that vulnerability is a strength, not a weakness. Opening up about your struggles, fears, and aspirations allows others to see your authentic self and provide the support you need. It takes courage to be vulnerable, but it can lead to deeper connections and more meaningful relationships.

Take the initiative to communicate your needs and express the specific support you are seeking. People may not always know how to help unless you tell them what you need. Be proactive in seeking out resources and opportunities that can aid you in your personal and educational development.

Remember that support may come in various forms, and it is essential to find what works best for you. Some individuals may benefit from one-on-one mentorship, while others thrive in group settings. Explore different avenues of support and find what resonates with you.

Finally, be patient and persistent in seeking the support you need. It may take time to find the right connections and build relationships based on trust and understanding. Keep reaching out and advocating for yourself, knowing that you deserve the support and guidance that will help you thrive.

To My Fellow Foster Youth

In the journey of foster care, seek out the support that is available to you. Surround yourself with people who believe in your potential and are willing to walk alongside you. Remember that asking for help is an act of strength and self-care. Together with your support network, you can overcome challenges and fulfill your dreams.

Amplifying Your Voice

Recognize that your voice matters. Your experiences within the foster care system offer valuable insights and perspectives that can drive positive change. You have the power to advocate for yourself and for others who may not have found their voice yet. By sharing your story, speaking your truth, and being a catalyst for reform, you can make a significant impact.

Your voice carries the weight of authenticity. As someone who has lived through the foster care system, you possess firsthand knowledge of its challenges, triumphs, and areas for improvement. Your unique perspective can bring about a deeper understanding and empathy among policymakers, advocates, and the general public.

Advocating for yourself is not only an act of self-empowerment but also a way to pave the way for others who might face similar circumstances. Speaking up and sharing your experiences raises awareness about the issues that affect foster youth. Your voice can be a powerful force in dismantling stigmas and stereotypes, promoting understanding, and fostering positive change.

Take the opportunity to share your story in safe and supportive spaces. This can be through public speaking engagements, writing, social media, or participating in advocacy groups. Your personal narrative has the potential to inspire and educate others, helping them see the human side of the foster care system and the individuals it impacts.

When advocating for change, it is essential to stay informed about the policies and practices that affect foster youth. Educate yourself about the existing laws, regulations, and support systems in place. This knowledge will strengthen your arguments and enable you to propose practical solutions to the issues at hand.

Collaborate with like-minded individuals and organizations that share your goals and values. Join forces with foster care advocacy groups, nonprofits, or grassroots movements that are dedicated to improving the foster care system. Together, you can amplify your voice and create a more significant impact.

To My Fellow Foster Youth

Remember that change takes time, and progress may come in incremental steps. Always remain resilient and persistent in your advocacy efforts. Celebrate the small victories along the way and use them as fuel to keep pushing forward.

Your voice has the power to spark empathy, understanding, and meaningful change. Every time you share your story, you create an opportunity for others to connect with your experiences on an emotional level. This connection can inspire action, whether it is in the form of policy reform, increased funding for support services, or a shift in societal attitudes.

Know that your voice matters, and your perspective is valuable. Embrace the power of your voice to advocate for yourself, to shed light on the foster care system's challenges, and to be a catalyst for positive change. When you speak up and share your truth, you contribute to a society that is more compassionate, inclusive, and supportive of foster youth and their unique needs.

Against All Odds

Holding onto Hope

Finally, in the midst of life's challenges and adversities, always hold onto hope. Hope is a powerful force that can propel you forward, even in the darkest of times. It is the belief in the possibility of a brighter future, where your dreams can become a reality.

Hope serves as an anchor that keeps you grounded and focused on the positive aspects of life. It provides the strength and resilience needed to overcome obstacles and persevere in pursuit of your goals. Even when faced with setbacks or disappointments, hope can give you the motivation to keep moving forward.

Surround yourself with positive influences that uplift and inspire you. Seek out individuals who believe in you and your potential. Their support and encouragement can fuel your hope and remind you of the extraordinary capabilities that reside within you. Remember that you are not alone on this journey, and there are people who want to see you succeed.

Nurture your passions and interests. Engage in activities that bring you joy and fulfillment. Pursue your dreams with determination and enthusiasm. Cultivate a mindset that embraces possibilities and sees challenges as steppingstones towards growth.

To My Fellow Foster Youth

By nourishing your passions, you keep the flame of hope burning brightly within you.

We must acknowledge that hope does not mean denying or ignoring the realities of life. Adversities will come your way, and you may encounter obstacles that seem insurmountable. However, hope allows you to approach these challenges with resilience and a belief that things can get better.

Believe in your own potential and the power of your dreams. Recognize that you have unique talents, strengths, and abilities that can contribute to creating a brighter future. Trust in your capacity to learn, grow, and make a positive impact on the world around you. Your dreams are not mere fantasies but visions of what can be achieved through dedication and perseverance.

Hold onto hope, even when circumstances seem bleak. Remember that life is full of possibilities, and change is always possible. Allow hope to guide your actions and decisions, leading you towards a future filled with purpose, fulfillment, and success.

In moments of doubt or uncertainty, remind yourself of the progress you have already made. Reflect on past achievements and the hurdles you have overcome. Draw strength from these experiences and let them fuel your hope for what lies ahead.

Hope is a choice that you can make every day. It is an attitude of optimism and resilience that can transform your outlook on life. By embracing hope and holding onto it steadfastly, you create a positive mindset that can attract opportunities and inspire others to do the same.

Always hold onto hope, for it is a beacon that illuminates the path ahead. Let hope be the driving force that propels you forward, even in the face of adversity. Believe in the extraordinary potential within you, nurture your passions, and never lose sight of the brighter future that awaits.

Chapter 9: To Foster Parents Everywhere

Earlier, I referenced three families who had a lasting impact on my life: The Wyatts, who took me into their home after my stint at the temporary shelter, the Stokes/Burts, who showed me what being a tight knit family was all about, and the Rashidis, who took me under their wing during my journey through college. They had a lasting impact because of their intentionality, care, and willingness to love me. As a child navigating the tumultuous foster care system, that was all I needed. If you are a foster parent or you want to become a foster parent, I want you to know that you have an enormous impact on the children who are living with you. And too, a responsibility to provide them with stable, compassionate care.

Foster parents and mentors, like the Wyatts, the Stokes/Burts, and the Rashidis, serve as beacons of hope and stability in the lives of children who have experienced adversity and uncertainty. By opening your heart and home, you create a safe harbor where these children can find solace, heal from their past, and grow into their full potential. Your intentionality, care, and willingness to love makes a lasting impact on their lives.

As a former child in the foster care system, I can attest to the significance of a stable and nurturing foster home. The relationships I formed with my foster parents provided me with the love, support, and guidance that I desperately needed. They were there for me during the ups and downs, offering a listening ear, a shoulder to lean on, and words of encouragement. Their presence made a profound difference in my life.

By stepping into the role of a foster parent, you take on the responsibility of providing stable, compassionate care to these vulnerable children. Your dedication and commitment can shape the trajectory of their lives, offering them a chance to heal from past traumas, develop resilience, and thrive in a nurturing environment.

 **Your actions leave an indelible mark on their hearts and minds, instilling a sense of security, self-worth, and belonging.**

Foster Parents Everywhere

It's important to recognize the power of your role as a foster parent. Being intentional in your interactions, demonstrating empathy, and creating a loving environment, helps these children overcome their challenges and flourish. Your commitment to their well-being and growth can have a ripple effect, extending beyond their time in foster care and positively influencing their future relationships and life choices.

In this chapter, I've outlined a few sections to help you navigate the life of a foster parent. Each section provides valuable insights and practical strategies to support you in your journey. Embracing the responsibility of foster parenting and appreciating the impact you can have will make a profound difference in the lives of these precious children. Together, we can create a brighter future for them, one filled with love, stability, and endless possibilities.

Understanding the Needs of Foster Children

To be an effective foster parent, it is crucial to understand the unique needs and challenges that foster children often face. These children have experienced various forms of trauma, instability, and loss, which can profoundly impact their emotional, developmental well-being. By gaining insight into their needs and providing appropriate support, you can create a nurturing environment that helps foster children heal, grow, and thrive. In this section, we will explore the key aspects of understanding the needs of foster children.

1. Healing from Trauma:

- Many foster children have experienced trauma, such as abuse, neglect, or separation from their biological families.
- Understanding the effects of trauma and how it manifests in their behavior is crucial in providing appropriate support.
- Foster children may exhibit symptoms of anxiety, depression, withdrawal, aggression, or difficulty forming trusting relationships.
- Creating a safe and predictable environment, offering patience, empathy, and access to therapeutic resources can aid in their healing process.

2. Stability and Consistency:

- Stability is a fundamental need for foster children who have faced multiple disruptions and uncertainties in their lives.
- Consistency in daily routines, expectations, and boundaries can provide a sense of security and help them develop a sense of trust.

- Foster parents can work closely with caseworkers and other professionals to ensure consistent care, minimize disruptions, and maintain a stable living environment.

3. Emotional Support and Validation:

- Foster children often carry complex emotions related to their past experiences and the challenges of being in foster care.
- Offering empathy, active listening, and validating their feelings can create a safe space for them to express themselves.
- Encouraging healthy emotional expression and teaching coping skills can help foster children navigate their emotions and develop resilience.

4. Educational Support:

- Foster children may experience educational disruptions due to frequent placement changes or lack of educational resources.
- Advocating for their educational needs, providing tutoring or additional support, and maintaining communication with their teachers can enhance their academic success.
- Creating a positive learning environment at home and encouraging their educational aspirations can empower foster children to reach their full potential.

5. Connection with Biological Families:
- Recognizing the importance of maintaining connections with their biological families is crucial for foster children's well-being.
- Supporting visitations, encouraging positive communication, and fostering a respectful understanding of their family background can help them maintain a sense of identity and belonging.
- Collaboration with caseworkers and birth families, when appropriate, can contribute to a holistic approach that supports the child's best interests.

Understanding the needs of foster children is a vital aspect of being a nurturing and supportive foster parent. By acknowledging their unique backgrounds, experiences, and challenges, you can provide the care and support necessary for their healing and growth. Emphasizing stability, consistency, emotional support, educational opportunities, and connection with their biological families creates an environment that enables foster children to thrive. Remember, every child is different, and their needs may vary. By remaining open, adaptable, and committed to their well-being, you can make a profound difference in their lives, offering them a brighter future filled with love, stability, and hope.

Building Trust and Attachment

Building trust and forming secure attachments are essential components of foster parenting. For foster children who have experienced trauma, instability, and multiple transitions, developing a sense of trust and building healthy attachments can be challenging. As a foster parent, you play a crucial role in creating a safe and nurturing environment that fosters trust and promotes secure attachments. In this section, we will explore strategies and principles for building trust and attachment with foster children.

1. Establishing a Safe and Predictable Environment:

- Foster children need a safe and predictable environment where they can feel secure and develop trust.
- Maintain consistent routines, boundaries, and expectations to provide a sense of stability.
- Create a calm and nurturing physical space that reflects their individuality and offers a sense of belonging.

2. Patience, Empathy, and Active Listening:

- Foster children may carry emotional wounds and may struggle to trust others.
- Practice patience and empathy as they navigate their emotions and behaviors.

- Practice patience and empathy as they navigate their emotions and behaviors.
- Engage in active listening to understand their perspectives and validate their feelings.
- Demonstrate genuine care, respect, and understanding to build a foundation of trust.

3. Building Rapport and Connection:

- Foster children often benefit from positive and meaningful connections with adults.
- Engage in activities that promote bonding, such as shared hobbies, outings, or family meals.
- Show sincere interest in their lives, strengths, interests, and cultural background.
- Find opportunities for quality one-on-one time to foster a sense of individual connection.

4. Consistency and Reliability:

- Consistency in your actions and reliability in keeping commitments are vital for building trust.
- Follow through on promises, be punctual, and communicate openly and honestly.
- Demonstrate that you are a dependable and trustworthy caregiver.

5. Empowerment and Collaboration:

- Involve foster children in decision-making processes, whenever appropriate and feasible.

- Encourage their opinions and choices within appropriate boundaries.
- Collaborate with them to set goals, solve problems, and make plans for their future.
- Foster a sense of empowerment and autonomy, promoting their self-confidence and self-esteem.

6. Seek Professional Support:

- Recognize that building trust and attachment can be complex, especially for children who have experienced trauma.
- Consult with professionals, such as therapists or social workers, who can provide guidance and support.
- Attend training sessions or workshops to enhance your understanding of attachment and trauma-informed care.

Building trust and forming secure attachments with foster children requires patience, empathy, and a commitment to their well-being. When I think back to my best experiences in foster care, it was the intentionality and consistency of foster parents that made all the difference. If a child knows you have their back, that you care for them, and you want a relationship with them, the dynamics will change. Sure, they may still struggle with behavior or trust, but they know that you are providing a loving and nurturing environment.

Collaborating with the Child's Support Team

Collaborating with the child's support team is a crucial aspect of foster parenting. Through open communication, active engagement, and genuine interest in the child's well-being, foster parents can create a supportive network to nurture their development. Drawing from my own experiences with the Wyatt family, who held me accountable, attended parent-teacher conferences, and showed a vested interest in my school day, I can attest to the importance of collaboration in fostering positive outcomes for foster children.

1. Open Communication and Information Sharing:

- Foster parents should establish open lines of communication with caseworkers, therapists, and educators involved in the child's life.
- Share relevant information regarding the child's background, experiences, strengths, and challenges.
- Actively participate in meetings, such as case reviews or Individualized Education Program (IEP) meetings, to contribute to the child's plans and goals.
- Provide updates on the child's progress, milestones, and any concerns that may arise.

2. Active Engagement in Education:

- Attend parent-teacher conferences, school events, and meetings with school staff to stay informed about the child's academic progress.
- Collaborate with educators to develop strategies and accommodations that address the child's unique needs.
- Advocate for necessary support services, such as tutoring, counseling, or special education resources, when appropriate.
- Share your observations and insights about the child's strengths, interests, and challenges with the educational team.
- Celebrate the wins! If your foster child achieves a goal—no matter how small—celebrate it with them. Put it on the fridge, get a special treat, and celebrate.

3. Supporting Therapeutic Interventions:

- Foster children often benefit from therapeutic interventions to address trauma, emotional well-being, and behavioral challenges.
- Collaborate with therapists and mental health professionals to reinforce therapeutic goals and strategies at home.
- Attend therapy sessions when appropriate and actively participate in recommended activities or exercises.

- Provide a consistent and supportive environment that complements the therapeutic work being done.

4. Encouraging Birth Family Connections:

- Recognize the importance of maintaining connections with the child's birth family, when appropriate and in the child's best interest.
- Collaborate with caseworkers to facilitate visitations, phone calls, or other forms of contact.
- Share relevant information about the child's progress, achievements, and challenges with the birth family, as appropriate and allowed.
- Foster an environment of respect and understanding for the child's family background and culture.

5. Accountability and Support:

- When the report card comes home, be supportive. Go through it together, talk about the highlights, and then address the opportunities for growth. Listen to their perspective.
- Set clear expectations and boundaries for behavior and academic performance.
- Maintain regular communication with the child, discussing their achievements, challenges, and goals.
- Provide guidance, encouragement, and support to help the child overcome obstacles and reach their full potential.

Supporting Educational Success

If your foster child is in a traditional setting, their school day likely takes up a significant portion of their day, lasting for upwards of eight hours. As a foster parent, you may only have three to four hours in the evenings to spend with them. While it's essential to make the most of that time, it's equally crucial to recognize the significance of their school day. Therefore, being deeply invested in your foster child's educational success becomes paramount.

1. Create a Supportive Learning Environment:

- Foster a positive and supportive atmosphere at home that encourages learning and academic growth.
- Set up a dedicated study area with necessary materials and resources that cater to their individual needs.
- Establish consistent routines and study schedules to provide structure and promote focus.
- Celebrate their accomplishments and provide gentle guidance during challenges to foster a love for learning.

2. Develop Open Communication with Teachers:

Build strong relationships with your foster child's teachers to stay informed about their academic progress and challenges.

- Attend parent-teacher conferences and actively engage in regular communication with educators.
- Share important information about your foster child's background, strengths, and challenges to help teachers better understand their unique needs.
- Collaborate with teachers to develop strategies and interventions that support their educational journey.

3. Advocate for Individualized Support:

- Recognize that each foster child has unique educational needs and advocate for individualized support when necessary.
- Participate in meetings such as Individualized Education Program (IEP) meetings to ensure their needs are addressed.
- Share your observations and insights about your foster child's strengths and challenges to contribute to the development of tailored strategies and accommodations.
- Work closely with educators and support staff to ensure they receive the necessary resources and interventions for academic success.

4. Foster a Love for Learning:

- Encourage and nurture your foster child's love for learning by exposing them to diverse educational experiences and opportunities.

- Provide access to age-appropriate books, educational games, and activities that spark their curiosity and creativity.
- Engage in educational outings, such as museum visits or cultural events, to broaden their horizons and stimulate their enthusiasm for learning.
- Support their interests and talents, allowing them to explore their passions and develop a lifelong love for learning.

5. Celebrate Achievements and Progress:
- Celebrate your foster child's achievements and progress to motivate and inspire them along their educational journey.
- Recognize their efforts, no matter how small, to instill a sense of pride and self-confidence.
- Offer praise for their hard work and resilience, encouraging them to set goals and strive for continuous improvement.
- Use rewards, special treats, or outings as incentives to reinforce the value of their educational success.

Being deeply invested in your foster child's educational success is crucial, considering the limited time you have with them outside of their school day. Creating a supportive learning environment, developing open communication with teachers, advocating for individualized support, fostering a love for learning, and celebrating achievements and progress, will make a significant impact on their educational journey. Through your dedication and involvement, you empower your foster child to overcome challenges, explore their potential, and develop a lifelong passion for learning. Remember, your investment in their education sets the stage for their future success.

Celebrate Achievements and Progress

It's important to promote cultural understanding and embrace your foster child's identity. Everyone comes from different backgrounds and has unique experiences, and as a foster parent, you can play a crucial role in helping your foster child appreciate their cultural heritage and develop a strong sense of self. Here are some ways you can foster cultural competency and identity:

1. Respect and Value Differences:
- Show respect for your foster child's cultural background, traditions, and beliefs.
- Encourage open conversations about their heritage, customs, and experiences.
- Foster an environment where diversity is celebrated, and differences are valued.
- Avoid stereotypes and judgments, promoting acceptance and understanding.

2. Learn Together:
- Take the initiative to learn about your foster child's cultural background.
- Read books, watch movies, or explore online resources that highlight their heritage.
- Engage in activities that allow you to experience their culture firsthand, such as cooking traditional meals or attending cultural events.
- Encourage your foster child to share their knowledge and teach you about their traditions.

3. Incorporate Cultural Celebrations:
- Celebrate important cultural holidays and traditions together as a family.
- Involve your foster child in planning and preparing for these celebrations.
- Attend community events or connect with local cultural organizations to expose your foster child to their cultural community.
- Embrace the opportunity to learn from others and create meaningful connections.

4. Support Identity Exploration:
Help your foster child explore and develop their personal identity.
Encourage self-reflection and provide a safe space for them to express their thoughts and emotions.

- Support their exploration of different aspects of their identity, including cultural, racial, and ethnic backgrounds.
- Validate their feelings and experiences, helping them develop a strong and positive sense of self.

5. Connect with Support Networks:

- Seek out support networks that can help your foster child connect with their cultural community.
- Look for local cultural organizations, community centers, or mentorship programs that can provide guidance and support.
- Encourage your foster child to build relationships with peers who share their cultural background.
- Help them maintain connections with their biological family, if appropriate, to strengthen their cultural ties.

6. Address Bias and Prejudice:

- Address any bias or prejudice that your foster child may encounter.
- Teach them about diversity, inclusion, and social justice.
- Encourage critical thinking and empathy, helping them navigate and challenge stereotypes and discrimination.
- Foster an environment where they feel safe to discuss and ask questions about issues related to bias and prejudice.

Foster Parents Everywhere

Promoting cultural understanding and embracing your foster child's identity is essential for their overall well-being and sense of belonging. Respecting and valuing differences, learning together, incorporating cultural celebrations, supporting identity exploration, connecting with support networks, and addressing bias and prejudice, can cultivate an inclusive and nurturing environment. Remember, embracing diversity and cultural competency not only enriches your foster child's life but also fosters a more inclusive and compassionate society for everyone.

Managing Challenging Behaviors

As a foster parent, it's common to face challenging behaviors from your foster child. These behaviors can range from tantrums and defiance to withdrawal or aggression. While it can be tough to navigate these moments, there are strategies you can use to manage and support your foster child effectively. Here are some practical tips to help you through those challenging times:

1. Stay Calm and Patient:
- It's natural to feel frustrated or overwhelmed but try your best to remain calm and composed.

- Take deep breaths and remind yourself that the behavior is not a personal attack.
- Responding with patience and understanding can help de-escalate the situation.

2. Establish Clear Expectations and Boundaries:
- Set clear and age-appropriate expectations for your foster child's behavior.
- Communicate these expectations calmly and consistently.
- Establish boundaries that promote safety, respect, and healthy interactions.
- Reinforce these boundaries with gentle reminders and consistent consequences.

3. Use Positive Reinforcement:
- Catch your foster child exhibiting positive behaviors and acknowledge them with praise and encouragement.
- Offer specific and genuine compliments to reinforce their efforts.
- Use rewards, such as stickers or privileges, to motivate and reinforce positive behavior.
- Celebrate small victories and progress to boost their self-esteem.

4. Implement Behavior Management Techniques:

- Use behavior management techniques, like redirection and distraction, to shift their focus away from negative behaviors.
- Offer choices to empower them and give them a sense of control.
- Use time-outs or quiet spaces as a calm-down strategy when necessary, ensuring they understand it's not a punishment but a chance to regain composure.
- Use positive language and avoid engaging in power struggles.

5. Foster Emotional Connection and Empathy:

- Validate your foster child's feelings and emotions, even if you don't agree with their behavior.
- Listen actively and show empathy by acknowledging their perspective.
- Help them identify and express their emotions in a healthy and constructive way.
- Engage in activities that nurture emotional connection, such as reading together or engaging in hobbies they enjoy.

6. Seek Professional Support:

- If challenging behaviors persist or escalate, seek guidance from professionals such as therapists, counselors, or social workers.

- They can provide valuable insights and offer strategies tailored to your foster child's specific needs.
- Attend therapy sessions or parenting support groups to learn new techniques and connect with others facing similar challenges.

At the end of the day, being invested in your foster child is no different from being invested in your biological child's life. As a foster parent, it's essential to recognize that the love, support, and dedication you provide should be no less than what you would offer to your biological children. While the circumstances may be different, the impact you can have on your foster child's life is just as profound. When you embrace this mindset, you help create a nurturing and transformative environment that allows your foster child to thrive and reach their full potential.

Conclusion: Hope Beyond Adversity

As we come to the end of this memoir, Against All Odds: Overcoming Adversity in Foster Care, the journey we have embarked on together has been one of heartache, resilience, and ultimately, hope. Through the vivid and unfiltered accounts of my experiences, we have delved into the hidden realities of a flawed foster care system and the profound impact it has on the lives of countless children. But amidst the darkness, we have witnessed the extraordinary power of perseverance and the indomitable spirit that resides within us all.

From the blur of sirens and flashing lights that marked the beginning of my journey, to the relentless shuffling between temporary shelters and unfamiliar faces, the obstacles seemed insurmountable. The scars of abuse, neglect, and trauma threatened to define me, to extinguish the flickering flame within. Yet, it was precisely in those moments of despair that the fire burned brightest, refusing to be snuffed out.

Against All Odds

Dreams became my sanctuary, an escape from the pain and a beacon of possibility in a world that often felt cold and unforgiving. They became the compass that guided me through the labyrinth of foster homes, an anchor amid the turmoil. Clinging to those dreams, I discovered the strength to rise above the circumstances, to rewrite the narrative that sought to confine me.

This memoir stands as a testament to the power of the human spirit, to the resilience that can be found even in the deepest recesses of our souls. It is a testament to the strength we possess to overcome adversity, to heal, and to triumph. Through sharing my story, I hope to inspire others who have faced similar challenges, to let them know that they are not alone and that their dreams hold the power to transform their lives.

But beyond the personal narrative, this memoir serves a greater purpose—a call to action. It shines a light on the flaws within the foster care system and invites us to examine the ways in which we can effect change. It urges us to advocate for the recruitment and support of loving, stable foster families, for comprehensive services that address the unique needs of foster children, and for collaboration between agencies and schools to ensure educational stability and support.

Conclusion: Hope Beyond Adversity

The foster care system, in its current state, often fails to provide the nurturing and stable environment that children so desperately need. It is marked by systemic issues such as overcrowded homes, high caseloads for social workers, and limited resources for mental health and educational support. These shortcomings perpetuate the cycle of trauma and instability, making it difficult for foster children to break free from the chains that bind them.

To create a future of opportunity and support for foster children, we must collectively strive for change. Change starts with the recruitment and training of foster families who can provide the love, stability, and guidance that these children need to thrive. Foster parents should be equipped with the knowledge and resources necessary to address the unique challenges faced by foster children, including trauma-informed care, therapeutic techniques, and access to mental health services.

Comprehensive services must be made available to foster children to address their multifaceted needs. This includes access to quality healthcare, mental health counseling, and educational support tailored to their individual circumstances. The foster care system should prioritize the provision of wraparound services that consider the holistic development of each child, ensuring that they receive the necessary support to heal, grow, and succeed.

Collaboration between agencies, schools, and communities is paramount to the success of foster children. Communication and coordination among these entities can ensure educational stability, as well as facilitate the sharing of information and resources that can support foster children's well-being. By working together, we can create a seamless network of support that spans across all aspects of a foster child's life, from their home to their school, and beyond.

Furthermore, it is essential to invest in training and professional development for social workers and educators who work with foster children. By equipping these professionals with the knowledge and skills necessary to support the unique needs of foster children, we can enhance the quality of care and education provided to these vulnerable individuals.

As we conclude this book, may it be a reminder that our stories have the power to reshape the world. Let us carry the embers of hope, stoked by our collective determination, to create a foster care system that provides solace, stability, and opportunity for every child. Together, we can build a future where no child faces the shadows alone, and where the triumph of the human spirit becomes a guiding light for generations to come.

Resources

Life Lessons for Foster Youth

1. Relationships and Reputation: As you grow and develop, understand that no one gets anywhere in life on their own merit. Foster and develop relationships with those that will have the most impact on your life. That means interacting and getting to know your social workers, foster parents, teachers, and school guidance counselors. Your relationships with these people will be beneficial towards your future goals. Establish a reputation as someone who works hard, is disciplined, and sets a positive example for others to follow. If your group of friends aren't ones that exhibit any of the aforementioned characteristics, then find other ones. If you hang out with problematic kids, you will be identified as one and will gain a reputation as one. The better your reputation, the more likely people will want to do things for you.

2. Life is 10% what happens to you and 90% how you react to it: For most of us in foster care, our parents abused us, they passed away, were on drugs or found unfit to care for us. No matter the reason, we ended up in the foster care system and it is up to us to make the best of a bad situation. I present to you the "tennis ball vs. egg". The fundamental difference between a tennis ball and an egg lies in their responses to impact or stress. When a tennis ball is dropped, it bounces back; it's resilient and can withstand repeated impacts without breaking. On the other hand, an egg is fragile; when dropped, it breaks easily and cannot recover its original form. In life, it's beneficial to be like a tennis ball, exhibiting resilience and the ability to bounce back from challenges or adversity. As foster youth, you face a unique set of challenges, including instability, feelings of loss or abandonment, and emotional turmoil. You have to learn to adapt to being in new living environments, with new foster parents, new case managers, new schools, on top of dealing the stress and anxiety of trying to be a kid. I will be the first one to tell you, there is nothing normal about being in foster care. It is not the optimal way to grow up as a child. You are often times under heavy supervision, with a ton of red tape that you have to go through, just to enjoy privileges that kids living with their parents get to every day. For some of you, the foster care system is a temporary pit stop until you can go back to your biological family. For others, you will remain in the system until you decide to emancipate. Within that time, you need to do your best at developing resilience. The quicker you become good at adapting to new situations, coping with changes, and finding that inner strength during tough times, the more successful you will become. Resilience, adaptability, and a positive attitude will allow you to find the skills needed to navigate the complexities of your specific situation and emerge a stronger, more mentally tough individual.

3. Your past does not define your future: Foster care might be a part of your life story, but it does not determine who you can become. You have the power to shape your own destiny and create a future filled with success and happiness. You have the power to make choices that will positively impact your life for years to come. This includes the food you eat and how many times you exercise per week, the group of friends you hang around, books you read, television shows you watch, all the way to the choices you make financially with any money you earn or receive.

4. Advocate for yourself: Learn to speak up for your needs, rights, and dreams. Be an active participant in your own life and advocate for the support and resources you require. Your voice matters, and you deserve to be heard. Enhance your communication skills to express needs, concerns, and goals clearly. This includes both verbal and written communication. Practice articulating your thoughts and feelings to caregivers, caseworkers, teachers, and others involved in your care. Learn the ins and outs about the foster care system, including its processes, policies, and key decision-makers. Knowledge is a powerful tool in advocating for your needs and rights.

5. Seek and accept help: It is not a sign of weakness to ask for assistance. Reach out to supportive adults, mentors, caseworkers, or support groups when you need guidance or support. Accepting help is a strength and a crucial part of your growth and well-being. There are people that want to see you be successful and will do anything within their power to see to it that you do so. Utilize any resources that they can provide and most importantly listen to them. Most of the adults in your life have been around the block and have dealt with some of the same issues you are going through. Seek their advice on how they would deal with certain situations so that you don't make the same mistakes over and over again.

6. Surround yourself with positive influences: Surround yourself with people who believe in you and your potential. Seek out mentors and role models who inspire and support you. Positive influences can uplift you during challenging times and help you stay focused on your goals. Surround yourself with friends that possess a good character and that are successful academically. Honor, respect, integrity, and discipline are the kind of qualities you should imitate as well as the qualities you should look for when selecting friends. Always do what is right when no one is looking. Choose the hard right over the easy wrong and you will quickly gain respect as a leader amongst your peers and your superiors.

7. Find a mentor: Cultivate relationships with individuals who genuinely care about your well-being. Surround yourself with a supportive network of friends, mentors, and professionals who can provide guidance, encouragement, and a listening ear. I met my mentors Kuumba and Lisa, during my freshman year of college in the fall of 2007, and 17 years later, I visit them every year for the holidays and keep extremely close contact with them. They went from being my mentors to becoming the mother and father figures I never had. They treat me like one of their own children and I love them as if they gave birth to me. Was it always like this? Absolutely not. There were times when I was hard-headed and didn't want to listen in my early-20s. Now that I am in my mid-30s, I value their input in any important decision I make and look to them for guidance when I don't have the answers to a problem. I hope you are able to find your "Kuumba and Lisa," and that they will speak life and inspiration into you the way they did for me.

8. Take care of yourself: Self-care is essential. Prioritize your physical, mental, and emotional well-being. Engage in activities that bring you joy, practice self-compassion, and prioritize your health. Taking care of yourself allows you to better navigate the challenges you may encounter. Get active; ask your foster parents and caseworker to get you involved in sports, a weightlifting gym, or something that keeps you physically fit. We live in a time where everyone wants to sit in front of a TV and play video games all day. Don't be that person; get outside and get active.

9. Education is a powerful tool: Embrace the opportunity to pursue education. It opens doors and equips you with knowledge and skills that can empower you to create a better future. Take advantage of available educational resources and strive for academic success. You may not understand it now but the more seriously you take your education, the easier it will be when it comes time to apply for your first adult job. Employers want to see how disciplined you were in your studies as a way to gauge your potential within their company. Work hard in school now so that a few years from now, you will have your pick of roles and you can have the career that you want.

10. Embrace your identity: Your background and experiences make you unique. Embrace your identity, including your cultural heritage and personal history. Celebrate your strengths and recognize the value that diversity brings to the world. Explore and celebrate your cultural, ethnic, or religious heritage. This could involve participating in cultural events, learning about your ancestral history, or engaging in cultural practices. This connection can provide a sense of belonging and pride in your roots. Also, start to find a something that you are passionate about. Explore and engage in activities that resonate with your personal interests, whether it's art, music, sports, or any other hobby. This exploration not only fosters a sense of self but also helps in developing a personal identity separate from your situation.

11. Learn from setbacks: In life, you must be able to contend with humiliation, broken dreams, sadness, and loss. Use these moments as opportunities for growth and learning. Embrace resilience and develop the ability to bounce back from challenges. Remember that failure is not permanent, and it can often lead to new opportunities and greater success. Dealing with setbacks often involves managing emotions such as frustration, disappointment, or sadness. Learning to navigate these emotions effectively can enhance emotional intelligence, leading to better relationships and self-awareness. Overcoming challenges and learning from setbacks will build confidence. Each time you successfully navigate a difficult situation, your belief in your abilities is strengthened. Most importantly, by reflecting on setbacks, you are able to gain insight into your decision-making processes. This reflection can lead to more thoughtful and informed decisions in the future which will be the catalyst for your success once you are no longer in the foster care system.

12. Believe in yourself: You will often face significant challenges that can impact your self-esteem and self-belief. Have faith in your abilities and believe in your capacity to overcome obstacles and achieve your goals. Trust in your own resilience and inner strength. With self-belief, you can overcome challenges and create a fulfilling life. I encourage each of you to practice positive affirmations and constructive self-talk. Replacing negative thoughts with positive ones can significantly boost self-confidence and belief in your own abilities. If you enjoy writing, start a daily or weekly journal. This can help you reflect on your thoughts and feelings, understand yourself better, and build a positive self-image.

13. Set Goals: Goals can provide you with direction and a sense of purpose. They act as a roadmap, putting you on the path that you want to follow. Goals help with decision-making that align with your aspirations. Goals will give you a reason to stay focused and committed, even in the face of challenges. Having clear objectives helps foster a sense of determination and perseverance. Overcoming challenges in the pursuit of goals will build resilience, confidence, and a sense of accomplishment, fostering a positive self-image. Talk about things that you want to accomplish with your social workers, foster parents, and teachers. Whether these are monthly, quarterly, or yearly goals, write them down, stick to them, and be amazed at your own growth and development.

14. Give back: As you grow and succeed, consider giving back to your community or helping others who may be going through similar experiences. Your journey can inspire and support others, and by making a difference, you contribute to creating a better world. This book that you are reading is my way of giving back to you. Maybe one day you will decide to write your own book, develop a YouTube channel, or create a charity that donates proceeds to foster youth in your area. The important thing is not to forget the ones that are coming after you that are going through the same issues you went through. Your words of inspiration could mean the world to someone.

15. Never lose hope: Hold onto hope even in challenging times. It can be a powerful force that propels you forward. Believe in the possibility of a brighter future and never lose sight of your dreams. With hope, determination, and perseverance, you can achieve extraordinary things. If I can overcome the death of my mother, severe physical and mental abuse, 25+ foster homes, 13 different schools, and a host of other setbacks, I absolutely believe you can overcome your own adversity and setbacks. Be an inspirational story that can be shared with the world.

Remember, these life lessons are meant to serve as guidance and inspiration. Each individual's journey is unique, and it's important to adapt and apply these lessons in ways that resonate with your own experiences and aspirations.

Building Your Independent Living Skills

As a foster youth, developing independent living skills is vital as you transition into adulthood. These skills empower you to navigate the challenges of daily life, make informed decisions, and achieve self-sufficiency. Here are some key areas to focus on as you build your independent living skills:

1. Taking Charge of Your Finances:
- Budgeting: Learn how to create and maintain a budget, track expenses, and set financial goals. This will help you manage your money wisely.
- Banking: Understand the basics of opening a bank account, managing transactions, and using online banking services.

- Saving: Discover the importance of saving money, setting aside emergency funds, and exploring options like savings accounts or investment opportunities.
- Understanding Credit: Learn about credit scores, credit reports, and responsible borrowing. Knowing how to manage credit will help you make smart financial decisions.

2. Managing Your Housing and Household:

- Finding Housing: Seek resources on searching for affordable housing options, understanding lease agreements, and knowing your tenant rights.
- Rent and Utility Payments: Learn how to manage monthly rent payments, utilities, and other household expenses responsibly.
- Home Maintenance: Acquire skills for basic home maintenance tasks, such as cleaning, organizing, and handling minor repairs.
- Meal Planning and Cooking: Discover tips for meal planning, grocery shopping on a budget, and basic cooking skills to feed yourself nutritiously.

3. Building Your Employment and Career Path:

- Job Readiness: Get equipped with resume writing, job searching, and interview skills. Look into vocational training programs, apprenticeships, and job placement services.

- Workplace Etiquette: Understand professional conduct, appropriate workplace communication, and conflict resolution skills.
- Career Exploration: Explore your interests, strengths, and skills to identify potential career paths. Seek resources for career counseling, vocational assessments, and educational opportunities.

4. Prioritizing Your Health and Well-being:

- Personal Health: Take care of your physical well-being by scheduling regular medical check-ups, adopting healthy eating habits, exercising, and practicing self-care.
- Mental Health: Understand the importance of managing stress, seeking counseling or therapy when needed, and accessing mental health resources available to you.
- Health Insurance: Learn about the process of obtaining and utilizing health insurance coverage, including Medicaid or other healthcare programs you may be eligible for.

5. Navigating Transportation and Mobility:

- Public Transportation: Familiarize yourself with public transportation options, including bus schedules, fares, and navigating routes.
- Driving and Car Ownership: If applicable, learn about obtaining a driver's license, understanding car insurance, and basic vehicle maintenance.

- Alternative Transportation: Explore biking, walking, carpooling, or rideshare services as alternative transportation options.

6. Knowing Your Legal Rights and Responsibilities:

- Understanding Your Legal Rights: Educate yourself about your legal rights and responsibilities, including knowledge of relevant laws and regulations.
- Legal Documentation: Learn how to obtain identification documents, such as social security cards, birth certificates, and driver's licenses.
- Legal Aid: Seek resources for accessing legal assistance or advocacy services when needed.

7. Time Management and Organization:

- Developing Schedules: Learn effective time management skills, including creating schedules, prioritizing tasks, and managing deadlines.
- Organization Skills: Discover strategies for organizing your personal belongings, paperwork, and important documents.

8. Building Social and Interpersonal Skills:

- Communication: Develop effective communication skills, including active listening, conflict resolution, and building positive relationships.

- Networking: Seek opportunities to build social networks, connect with mentors, and engage in community activities that align with your interests.

9. Becoming Your Own Advocate:
- Understand your rights and learn to speak up for your needs. Seek out necessary support and resources by navigating systems such as healthcare, education, and employment effectively.

Remember, building independent living skills takes time and practice. Take advantage of additional resources, workshops, or programs focused on independent living skills development. By equipping yourself with these essential skills, you can gain confidence, self-reliance, and a solid foundation for a successful transition into adulthood. You have the strength and resilience to overcome challenges and create a fulfilling life.

Mentorship Programs: Guiding You Towards Success

Mentorship programs can be invaluable resources for foster youth, connecting you with caring adult mentors who can offer guidance, support, and serve as positive role models on your journey. These programs your goals. Here's some information about mentorship programs and organizations that can be beneficial to you:

1. National Foster Youth Mentorship Programs:

- FosterClub: FosterClub is a national organization that offers a range of mentorship programs specifically tailored for foster youth. They connect you with mentors who have firsthand experience in the foster care system and can provide guidance and support.

- Big Brothers Big Sisters: This renowned organization has programs that match foster youth with caring adult mentors who provide one-on-one support, encouragement, and friendship.

2. Local Community Mentorship Programs:

- Local Foster Care Agencies: Reach out to your local foster care agency or child welfare department to inquire about mentorship programs available in your area. They may have partnerships with community organizations or volunteers who are dedicated to supporting foster youth.

- Nonprofit Organizations: Many nonprofit organizations focus on serving foster youth and offer mentorship programs. Research local organizations that specialize in foster care, education, or youth development to find mentorship opportunities that align with your interests and needs.

3.   College   and   Career-Based   Mentorship Programs:

- Higher Education Institutions: If you are pursuing higher education, check if your college or university provides mentorship programs for foster youth. These programs may pair you with mentors who can offer academic guidance, career advice, and support throughout your college journey.
- Professional Associations: Some professional associations have mentorship initiatives aimed at supporting young individuals entering specific fields. Explore professional organizations related to your career interests and inquire about mentorship opportunities available for foster youth.

4. Online Mentorship Platforms:

- iFoster: iFoster is an online platform that connects foster youth with mentors who can guide various aspects of life, such as education, employment, and independent living skills.
- Mentor.gov: The U.S. Department of Education's website, Mentor.gov, offers a directory of mentoring programs. While not specifically tailored to foster youth, it can be a helpful resource to find mentoring opportunities based on your location and interests.

When considering mentorship programs, keep in mind the specific support you are seeking and the qualities you value in a mentor. Look for programs that provide ongoing support, match you with mentors who share similar experiences or interests, and prioritize your well-being. Remember, mentorship is a two-way street, and you have valuable insights and strengths to bring to the relationship as well.

Reach out to the mentorship programs or organizations you are interested in to inquire about their application process, criteria for participation, and the types of support and guidance they offer. Take advantage of the opportunity to connect with caring mentors who can inspire you, share their wisdom, and help you navigate the challenges you may encounter. With the support of a mentor, you can build a strong foundation for success, unlock your potential, and thrive on your unique path.

Self-Care and Well-Being In the Foster Home

Taking care of your physical, mental, and emotional well-being is crucial while living within foster homes. It's important to prioritize self-care, manage stress effectively, and seek resources that promote your overall well-being. I know that your ability to control external factors is low, but you can pursue resources to control your wellbeing even when in various environments. Here are some strategies, resources, and recommendations to help you foster a positive mindset and nurture your physical, emotional health within foster homes:

1. Physical Well-being:

- Healthy Eating: Aim to incorporate nutritious foods into your meals and snacks. A balanced diet can provide you with the energy and nutrients your body needs. Seek guidance from your foster parents or caregivers on meal planning and explore resources like ChooseMyPlate. gov for healthy eating tips.
- Regular Exercise: Engage in physical activities that you enjoy and that align with your abilities. Exercise can boost your mood, reduce stress, and improve overall physical health. Find opportunities for physical activity within your foster home, such as going for walks, playing sports, or dancing.
- Adequate Sleep: Establish a consistent sleep routine and create a comfortable sleep environment within your foster home. Good sleep is vital for your physical and mental well-being. Talk to your foster parents or caregivers about establishing a calming bedtime routine and maintaining a regular sleep schedule.

2. Mental and Emotional Well-being:

- Self-Care Practices: Prioritize self-care activities that support your mental and emotional health. This can include engaging in hobbies, reading books, listening to music, or spending time in nature. Find activities that bring you joy and help you relax and recharge.

- Seek Emotional Support: Foster homes can provide a supportive environment, and it's essential to reach out to your foster parents or caregivers when you need emotional support. They can offer guidance, lend a listening ear, or help connect you with additional resources.
- Therapeutic Outlets: If needed, explore therapy or counseling options available to you. Your foster home or child welfare agency may have access to mental health professionals who can provide support and assist you in processing emotions or navigating challenges.

3. Resources for Well-being:

- Physical Fitness Programs: Inquire about physical fitness programs or sports activities available within your foster home or community. These programs can provide a structured approach to exercise and help you stay physically active.
- Online Resources: Explore websites, videos, or apps that offer guided exercises, yoga routines, or home workouts. Resources like Fitness Blender, Yoga with Adriene, or Nike Training Club provide a variety of free workout options that you can access from anywhere with an internet connection.

- Mental Health Apps: Consider utilizing mental health apps that offer guided meditations, stress management techniques, or tools for tracking your mood and emotions. Apps like Headspace, Calm, or MoodTools can provide support and resources for your mental and emotional well-being.

4. Building Supportive Relationships:

- Foster Care Support Groups: Seek out local or online support groups specifically for foster youth. These groups can provide a space to connect with others who share similar experiences, offer advice, and provide a sense of belonging.
- Open Communication: Foster a supportive and open line of communication with your foster parents or caregivers. Share your thoughts, concerns, and needs with them, as they may be able to provide guidance or connect you with appropriate resources.

Remember, self-care and well-being are ongoing practices, and it is important to find what works best for you within the context of your foster home. Advocate for your own well-being and communicate your needs to your foster parents or caregivers. By prioritizing your physical, mental, and emotional health, you can create a positive and nurturing environment within your foster home and support your overall well-being. You deserve care, support, and the opportunity to thrive within your current living situation.

Acknowledgements

To Kuumba and Lisa Rashidi...

In the autumn of 2007, amidst the golden hues of fall and the crisp beginnings of academic pursuits at Fort Valley State University, I found myself embarking on a new chapter far removed from the trials of my past. The decade preceding this moment had been a tumultuous journey through the foster care system, a period marked by uncertainty and the yearning for a place to call home. It was during this transformative time that I had the fortune of meeting two extraordinary individuals, Kuumba and Lisa Rashidi. Little did I know, they would become the beacon of light in my life, guiding me with unwavering love and compassion. This tribute is but a humble attempt to honor the monumental role they have played in my life, embodying the essence of parental love and mentorship that I had longed for.

Lisa Rashidi, a paragon of maternal grace, extended her warmth to me in a manner that was both healing and empowering. Her inherent motherly qualities were evident in every gesture, every word, and every moment of care she bestowed upon me. In her, I found a confidante, a guardian, and a source of endless encouragement. Lisa's determination to see me thrive was not just evident in her words but in her actions. She consistently made it her mission to ensure my well-being, seamlessly intertwining her love for her family with her devotion to her students and community. Lisa exemplified what it means to be an amazing wife to Kuumba and a phenomenal mother not only to her biological children, Oba and Makeda but also to me, treating me as her own with a love so genuine it transcended the boundaries of biology. Her strength, empathy, and unwavering support have been the cornerstone of my personal development, inspiring me to embrace life's challenges with grace and resilience.

Kuumba Rashidi stood as a testament to what it means to be a protector, a mentor, and a guiding light for not just his family but for all who had the privilege of crossing his path.

His embodiment of a great husband and father has been a constant source of inspiration for me, showcasing the profound impact of male mentorship in a young person's life. Kuumba's dedication to his family, his unwavering faith, and his commitment to service were the pillars upon which he built his legacy. His actions

Acknowledgements

spoke volumes, teaching me the invaluable lesson of responsibility, integrity, and the power of leading by example. Kuumba's influence has instilled in me a deep-seated desire to emulate these qualities when I have a family of my own, aspiring to be a beacon of strength, love, and guidance as he has been.

Together, Kuumba and Lisa Rashidi have been a formidable force of positivity, extending their nurturing hands not only to their immediate family but to the broader community. Their service to the church and unwavering faith in God have been a source of inspiration and a testament to their character. Their dedication to caring for foster youth and mentorship to students at Fort Valley State University, where we all share a common bond as alumni, highlights their commitment to uplifting others and fostering a sense of belonging and community.

Their home became a sanctuary for me, a place where I was embraced with open arms and where I could witness firsthand the beauty of a loving, functional family unit. The lessons learned and the love received within the walls of their home have been instrumental in shaping the person I am today. They taught me the value of compassion, the strength found in vulnerability, and the unmatched power of unconditional love.

Against All Odds

To Kuumba and Lisa Rashidi, words cannot fully capture the depth of my gratitude and the magnitude of my admiration for you both. You have been the mother and father figures I never had, guiding me through life's storms with a love so profound it has irrevocably changed my life for the better. As I reflect on the journey that has brought us together, I am filled with an overwhelming sense of gratitude for your presence in my life. Your unwavering support, your boundless love, and your exemplary lives have been the greatest gifts I could have ever received.

To Samuel Wright...

As I sit to pen this acknowledgment, a journey that spans over 17 years (man, time has flown) unfurls in the theater of my mind, a voyage that commenced in the crisp Autumn of 2007, beneath the embracing canopies of Fort Valley State University. It was here, amidst the hallowed halls of academia, that our paths converged, serendipitously drawn together on the same floor of the freshman dorms. Little did I know, this encounter was not merely a crossing of paths, but the forging of a bond destined to withstand the test of time.

Our initial acquaintance soon grew into a profound friendship, with destiny guiding us to share not just

Acknowledgements

spaces but countless memories as roommates. Samuel, in those formative years, you were an enigma to me - possessing a wisdom beyond your years, a thirst for knowledge that was unquenchable, and an even greater zeal to impart that knowledge. It wasn't long before I realized you were the brother I never knew I needed, a kindred spirit with whom I could talk sports, books, historical figures, music etc.

In an age where pretense often outweighs sincerity, you, Sam, chose a different path. Together, we navigated the complexities of youth, eschewing the limelight for the tranquility of our shared reclusiveness. Your focus never wavered from your pursuit of enlightenment, not just for yourself but for the world. Witnessing your growth, from those early days to seeing you adorned in the regalia of a master's graduate in education, has been one of my life's greatest honors.

Your journey didn't stop with your academic achievements. You delved into the realms of literature and journalism, penning books and articles that serve as a beacon for the African American community. Through your interviews and writings, you shed light on hip hop, social justice reform, and the intricate dynamics between Black men and women, educating and elevating us all.

Against All Odds

Yet, it was not just your public achievements that defined you. I had the privilege of standing by your side as you vowed eternal love to the woman of your dreams, a moment of joy that I cherish deeply. However, life's tapestry is woven with threads of both joy and sorrow. In the shadow of your mother's passing, I witnessed the strength of your spirit, your unwavering resolve to be the pillar your siblings needed, and the profound love and respect you harbored for your mother. Your eloquence in her honor was a testament to her legacy, a legacy that continues through you.

Samuel, as you step into your role as an Assistant Principal at Griffin High School, I am filled with pride. Your journey is a beam of hope and a testament to the impact one individual can have on the world. Your dedication to education and your unwavering commitment to fostering a love for learning in the hearts of young men and women are commendable. You are not just preparing them academically but shaping them to be conscientious citizens of the world.

Reflecting on our shared journey, from those early days in the dorms to the myriad milestones we've celebrated and the challenges we've faced, I am overwhelmed with gratitude. Your friendship has been a source of inspiration and unwavering support.

Acknowledgements

As I stand at the precipice of this new chapter in my life, with the ink drying on the pages of my book, I am reminded of the indelible mark you've left on my life and the lives of countless others. Your legacy lies not just in the knowledge you've imparted or the achievements you've amassed, but also in the lives you've touched, the minds you've enlightened, and the hearts you've warmed.

Samuel Hope Wright, to say that I am grateful to have you as my best friend would be an understatement. You have enriched my life in ways words can scarcely capture. As you continue your path, inspiring future generations, know that you carry with you my admiration and respect.

To my brother and dearest friend, I look forward to the many chapters yet to be written in your story. May your journey be filled with the same light, love, and wisdom that you've shared with all who have had the privilege of crossing your path.